# A SENSE OF DIRECTION

## William Gaskill

*faber and faber*

LONDON · BOSTON

First published in 1988
by Faber and Faber Limited
3 Queen Square London WCIN 3AU

Photoset by Parker Typesetting Service Leicester
Printed and bound in Great Britain by
Mackays of Chatham PLC, Chatham, Kent

*British Library Cataloguing in Publication Data*

Gaskill, William
A sense of direction.
1. Gaskill, William   2. Theatrical
producers and directors—Great Britain—
Biography
I. Title
792'.0233'0924    PN2598.G3/
ISBN 0-571-14838-7
ISBN 0-571-15250-3 Pbk

# Contents

# List of Illustrations

Avril Elgar, Marianne Faithfull, Glenda Jackson. (John Haynes)

9. Bond's *Lear*, Royal Court, 1971. The wall – Harry Andrews as Lear. (John Haynes)

10. Bond's *The Sea*, Royal Court, 1973: i The author in rehearsal, ii Simon Rouse, Mark McManus, Gillian Martell, Margaret Lawley, Coral Browne. (John Haynes)

11. David Hare's *Fanshen*, Joint Stock, 1975. Phillip McGough addresses the delegates. (John Haynes)

12. Heathcote Williams' *The Speakers*, Joint Stock, 1974. Tony Rohr as McGuinness. (John Haynes)

# Preface

This book had its origins in an article I wrote for *The Times* describing my memories of working at the Royal Court Theatre in the thirty years it has been the home of the English Stage Company. As I started to expand the idea into book length it became clear that I would have to tell something of my development as a director outside that wonderful old theatre in Sloane Square. The history of the ESC and the achievement of its founder director, George Devine, are already well documented. I did not want to plough through the same ground without giving an idea of how working at that theatre focused my whole approach to directing and gave me values that I have kept ever since.

The Court is a small theatre and it is impossible to work there without very close personal contact with everyone in the building – which certainly can't be said about the National Theatre or the Barbican. Much of the quality of its productions came from this intimacy and I hope the book reflects the same mixture of creative enterprise, emotional conflict, high-minded theory and straight gossip which made up our lives. I have written it almost entirely from memory and I am aware of huge gaps where I've failed to describe the contribution of every member of the staff whose involvement in the work of the Court gave it its identity. Let one example stand for all. At the beginning of my second season as Artistic Director I was rehearsing *Macbeth*. The first season had lost money and a great deal depended on the success of the production. The cleaning ladies were noisier than usual – or I was more nervous. I went to Elsie Fowler, the Court's housekeeper for many years, and said, 'Elsie, will you please keep your cleaners quiet.' She looked at me with the wisdom of someone who's seen it all before. 'All right, Bill, I'll do my best. I know it's a very important production for you.'

Without that understanding none of the achievements of the English Stage Company would have been possible. I would like to dedicate this book to all the people who have worked at the Court, for very little reward, because they felt it was important in their lives and in the development of vital theatre.

# I

# Beginnings; Tony Richardson

There was plenty of theatre in the West Riding of Yorkshire where I grew up during the Second World War: weekly repertory, amateur theatre, variety and touring shows. My father, a teacher at the local grammar school, thought they were 'dog-hanging shows' and would only take me to plays by Bernard Shaw, whom he considered an intellectual. It was my sisters, older than me and already at university in Leeds, who came home at weekends with descriptions of the ballets they had seen and who organized my first trips to the theatre, either at the Prince's or the Alhambra in Bradford, or even more exciting, at the Grand Theatre in Leeds. With the war British theatre had become decentralized; the Old Vic and Sadler's Wells had moved to Burnley under the direction of Tyrone Guthrie and tours were sent all over the North. And it was the Sadler's Wells Ballet in Robert Helpmann's *Hamlet* that gave me my first real theatre experience when I was twelve. Set to Tchaikovsky music, with Leslie Hurry's startling décor, a huge figure of Vengeance reaching across the backcloth, and the strange Freudian alternation of Gertrude and Ophelia in Hamlet's death-dream, it formed the basis of all my early productions. Helpmann had bridged the gap between dancing and acting and soon after played in Shakespeare's *Hamlet* for the Old Vic, co-directed by his lover Michael Benthall and Benthall's mentor Tyrone Guthrie, whose style of production

consisted of swirling banners and crowds in endless
movement.

The school I went to had separate boy and girl establish-
ments which were in the process of being combined. The girls'
school had an imaginative gym teacher, who had encouraged
the girls to create ballets of their own. I used to watch them
practising and gradually started to make suggestions as no one
was in charge. I soon took over the work and dictated my own
scenario, a wonderfully banal idea of a composer seated at the
piano and the notes coming to life (costumes after Christian
Bérard's for *Cotillon*). The music was the first movement of
Khachaturian's Piano Concerto. I was so pleased with my
creation that I choreographed the second movement in which
the music comes under strong nationalist influence and
decided to dance in it myself. I appeared in a fur cap and smock
as the Spirit of Russia, leaping around and handing out head-
scarves to the girls who were all in black and white. I think
classicism finally won. In later years Tony Richardson, who
also lived in Shipley, would remind me of this if he wanted to
cut me down to size. ('I saw you as the Spirit of Russia.')

Most of our theatre life revolved round the Civic Playhouse
in Bradford, one of the best amateur theatres in the country,
which was run by a professional director and former actress,
Esmé Church. Miss Church, as we called her, was a remarkable lady who was best known for her production of *As You
Like It* at the Old Vic with Edith Evans. She had been Guthrie's
right hand during the war years and when the Vic went back
to London she decided to make her career in the provinces.
Besides running the amateur theatre, which did premières of
plays by J. B. Priestley, James Bridie and Enid Bagnold which
the West End wouldn't touch, she ran a full-time professional
theatre school with Rudolf von Laban, one of the creators of
European modern dance. From the school developed an

imaginative children's theatre and a less successful touring company with guest performances by Ernest Milton as Shylock. The school drew on all the local talent including David Giles, who later became a director, Donald Howarth the writer, and actors like Bernard Hepton, Robert Stephens and Tom Bell. Esmé also ran a Saturday morning children's class which Billie Whitelaw and I attended. It was there that I first learned about directing and her very simple explanations of the texts of *Twelfth Night* and *The Tempest* have stayed with me ever since. Her vocal delivery I guess to have been modelled on Guthrie's; she spoke of 'gals' in her heavily adenoidal voice and had a slow walk back from giving notes. A large lady with wonderful old-gold hair and pale watery eyes, she dominated most of our lives.

One person she didn't dominate was Tony Richardson, the son of a pharmacist who lived down the road. His elongated figure and squeaky drawl singled him out in the artistic circles of the West Riding. He was iconoclastic about anything that was sentimental and old-fashioned. He would return from trips to London or Stratford with a description of the newest work by Peter Brook, the twenty-one-year-old whizz-kid, and pour scorn on all our sacred cows. On Edith Evans as Cleopatra: 'You should see her scrawny old chest in those dreadful Motley costumes.' Well, Edith was sixty and had left it a bit late for Cleopatra, but she was our greatest actress, we thought. Tony was dissatisfied with the opportunities at the Civic and formed his own group in Shipley, Young Theatre, of which I was a bit suspicious. A dancer whose career had been halted by polio used to give us a classical ballet class before each rehearsal. This was thought to be a necessary part of the development of the ensemble. Esmé came to the first production and said, 'Well, dear, it's the sort of thing we used to do in the hall for the servants.'

Soon after the formation of Young Theatre I won a state scholarship and rather unexpectedly got a place at Hertford College, Oxford. Tony had already won a scholarship to Wadham College and his father drove the two of us down or 'up' to Oxford in the autumn of 1948. Tony already knew what he wanted to do: to use his time at Oxford as a preparation for becoming a director. At that time there were no university drama departments (there still aren't at either Oxford or Cambridge) and the only way into the profession was through catching the eye of any managers you could persuade to come to your amateur productions, provided they were at one of the older universities. The example of Peter Brook was before us. When we arrived in Oxford we found it dominated by Kenneth Tynan in his purple suit. It was his last term. Tony said of him that his career was like a long letter home to his parents in Birmingham; but all our lives became like that. Tony was part of a generation elbowing its way into the Establishment by glorying in its provincial vitality. He proudly kept his Yorkshire accent while I was busy ironing mine out till I sounded – or thought I sounded – like the boys who had been to public school. Tony's ambition was enormous but he was never snobbish.

His influence on everyone who knew him was – and probably still is – devastating; creative and destructive, encouraging and disheartening, serious and flippant. Without him I would never have become a director. I was neither ambitious nor political, but I was swept along in his wake and buoyed up by his belief in me. My first attempt at directing was scenes from Dryden's *Marriage à-la-Mode* (after John Clements), with Sue Hopkinson, the writer, Shirley Williams, and John Gilbert, the Labour MP. Tony's was a scene from *Noah* (after Michel Saint-Denis). Soon after Tony brought his Young Theatre production of *Doctor Faustus* (after Peter Brook) to a church hall in the Cowley Road as if to say, 'We Northerners can do it just as well as you.' I played Lucifer in Nazi uniform; the Good Angel was dressed like Sara Allgood and the Bad Angel like Viven Leigh in *The Skin of Our Teeth*. The chorus were three girls in white shifts who did expressive movement like Isadora Duncan. There were interpolations from *Tamburlaine* to the accompaniment of Wagner.

Tony was soon President of the Oxford University Dramatic Society (OUDS) and I was struggling to find my own identity. One of the great influences on all of us was *Les Enfants du Paradis* with its panorama of French theatre life, the sexuality of Arletty, the wonderful ham acting of Pierre Brasseur and the mime of Jean-Louis Barrault. This was what theatre should be. On a visit to Paris I saw Louis Jouvet's productions of *Les Fourberies de Scapin* for Barrault, designed by Bérard, and of *Tartuffe* for his own company, designed by Braque, which seemed more stylish, more witty and more beautiful than anything I had ever seen. My last productions at Oxford were of Molière: *Le Misanthrope* in black and white, including the audience, with Christopher Fettes and Robert David Macdonald as the *petits marquis*; and *George Dandin* played in French on a bare stage in modern dress. Somehow I'd worked through all the directorial gimmicks in three years and ended up with the simplest and most concentrated theatrical statement. 'A theatre stage should have the maximum of verbal presence and the maximum of corporal presence,' Sam Beckett once wrote to Keith Johnstone and it was written on the wall of our office at the Royal Court.

Michel Saint-Denis had seen my production of part of *The Revenger's Tragedy* at Oxford and liked it and I'd tried to get George Devine to see my work in the hope of joining the Vic School. By the time I left Oxford the Vic School had been closed, so I had to look elsewhere. My father, having always been a francophile, scraped enough money together to send me to Paris where I studied mime with Étienne Decroux, (Déburau *père* in the film and the teacher of Barrault and Marcel Marceau), ballet with Lubov Egorova and acting with Tania Balachova. By the end of six months my money had run out and I'd seen every play in the repertoire of the Comédie Française, Giorgio Strehler's first *Servant of Two Masters* with Marcello Moretti, and Jean Vilar's work at the Théâtre National Populaire including my first Brecht, *Mère Courage*. Vilar's productions in the huge Palais de Chaillot were all on a bare stage, the *tréteau nu* of Jacques Copeau and Saint-Denis, but without their rostrums and staircases. Just the stage, strong, vivid costumes and good actors.

Guthrie too was moving towards his version of the Elizabethan stage. His production of *Henry VIII* at Stratford was done on a permanent set with bright lighting throughout. Night was conveyed by bringing lighted torches on to the stage. It was the first Shakespeare I had seen that had a political grasp of the play. Instead of providing a vehicle for the tragic figures of Katharine and Wolsey, Guthrie saw the whole play as a demonstration of Henry's ruthless power drive, creating the Reformation to further his own ends. Admittedly he outdid Shakespeare in the final arse-licking praise of Elizabeth, but it was Coronation year. Nowadays the production would be called Brechtian.

When my money ran out, I came back to England and went to see Guthrie. 'Don't stage manage,' he said. 'If you're any good at it, they'll never let you do anything else; if you're bad at it, they'll think you can't direct either.' I ignored his very good advice and went into weekly rep at Mansfield, Swindon, and Redcar. At a summer season at the Spa Theatre, Whitby, the leading man was David Baron, otherwise known as Harold Pinter. He told me he was a writer and very influenced by someone called Beckett. The work he described sounded like pretentious rubbish. The company was run by a local greengrocer, a staunch Methodist, whose wife saw Harold and the girl who was my assistant stage manager at it behind the sand dunes. The girl was instantly sacked. Harold protested and was told, 'Ah woan't have that hoor in my theatre, but you can stay.' Harold, to his everlasting credit, took the next train to London, and arrived penniless at King's Cross. I was in the middle of rehearsing *Fly Away Peter* (somehow I'd managed to squeeze a production from the management) in which Harold played the juvenile lead. He was also the leading man in the current show, a farce, and this was Wednesday night. The resident director, an experienced old actor, somehow managed to learn the whole part for the evening performance. His technique was interesting. He learned Act One before the show and nothing else. Then he learned Act Two in the first interval and Act Three in the second. He never faltered.

Nothing in the theatre today is quite like weekly repertory, though there is probably work even more slapdash. One was totally isolated in the routine of putting on plays; London was light-years away and none of the best actors had been in repertory. If they had, it was the classy three-weekly or even, my God, four-weekly, like Liverpool, Birmingham and Bristol. John Osborne describes the world wonderfully in his autobiography. The practices of Stanislavsky and his disciples were ridiculed. As for Saint-Denis and his masks and animal exercises – 'How frightful, my dear, they never know their lines.' I followed Osborne at Kidderminster whence I was eventually rescued by Tony Richardson offering me the job of assisting him on a production of *The Country Wife* at Stratford East. When that folded he somehow got me into Granada Television on the directors' course just as they were starting operations. By this time Tony had established himself as a television director and had met George Devine, whom he had cast in the adaptation of a Chekhov short story. They were already planning the Royal Court's first season.

# 2

# George Devine;
## *A Resounding Tinkle*

Tony and George became very close friends. The Old Vic
School and the triumvirate of George, Glen Byam Shaw and
Saint-Denis had broken up and George was looking for a new
direction in his life with the same vision and purpose. His roots
lay in the élitist classical theatre of John Gielgud, who in the
thirties had surrounded himself with all the most interesting
talent of his day and imported directors from Europe like
Theodore Komisarjevsky and Saint-Denis. In Tony George
found a new influence that was to push him towards new work
and a younger generation. George was a large man, though
not as fat as he had been in his youth; Tony was tall and thin.
They could have been Don Quixote and Sancho Panza except
that George was the dreamer, Tony the pragmatist.

They were soon planning to start a new theatre together.
Two years before the founding of the English Stage Company
they tried to start a company at the Royal Court in Sloane
Square, recently reopened after the bomb damage it had
suffered during the war, but finance fell through and the
season with it. My first experience of the wonderful old theatre
of Shaw and Granville-Barker was a production of *The
Comedy of Errors* with Ernest Milton as the Duke of Ephesus. In
their season George and Tony were not concentrating on
developing new writing but on the neglected European repertoire, what I call the Eric Bentley classics: Sternheim, Lorca,

Pirandello, etc. In fact the ESC was not founded by George and Tony but by three oddly assorted people: Lord Harewood, who wanted a drama company on the model of the English Opera Group, Ronald Duncan, who wanted a theatre that would present his poetic drama, and Oscar Lewenstein, who wanted a left-wing popular theatre like the Glasgow Unity he used to run. They offered George Devine the job as Artistic Director and he took it on the understanding that Tony would be his associate. The first season reflected the mixed taste of its founders and its directors.

I first met George in the Salisbury, a pub in St Martin's Lane, now a rather ill-tempered gay pub, then also gay but very theatrical; at that time the two were almost synonymous. George was a shy man whose shyness was covered by his rasping voice. He was wearing a duffel coat, and smoking one of his many pipes. He was only in his forties but his full wavy hair had turned white during the war and had changed him from the chubby comic actor of Gielgud's company into a much more patriarchal figure. He was never happy with this assumption; when I got to know him later he said, 'If I didn't have white hair and smoke a pipe nobody would pay any attention to me.' All I remember of our first meeting is a rather boring story he told of his time with the gunners during the war. 'We were working with an American regiment; when the guns didn't work we would say, "Check fire." The Americans would say, "What the hell do you mean 'Check Fire'? We always say, 'How come no egg.'"' Tony moved into George's house in Lower Mall, Hammersmith, in a flat now occupied by Peter Gill. The wardrobe department was in one of the bedrooms. I would sometimes stay there during my periods out of work and was an observer of the activity and discussion that preceded the first season in 1956. Tony found me a job directing a new play by a spinster from Hove at the old 'Q'

Theatre at Kew Bridge, after which he gave me pages of notes. Later he sponsored me as a trainee director at Granada Television and I did my first outside broadcast of *Zoo Time* with Desmond Morris at the London Zoo on 8 May 1956 before rushing off to Sloane Square to see the first night of *Look Back in Anger*.

Occasionally I would be drawn into discussions about design. Should there be a permanent set? I was full of neo-classical theories and said, 'I think you should have a permanent set made of stone.' 'Don't be so fucking stupid.' George came back from Berlin, where he'd been on tour with the Royal Shakespeare Company. He had seen the work of the Berliner Ensemble and met Brecht, who was already a mythical figure, though none of us had seen the work. 'What's it like?' we said. 'Well, you see, when there has to be a door there's just a door, but it's a real door and beautifully made.' I could see George's excitement about the theatre material and his love of craftsmanship. It's no coincidence that he shared his life with two designers: his wife, Sophie Harris, of Motley, and Jocelyn Herbert.

The story of the arrival of the script of *Look Back in Anger* and George's visit to John Osborne in his houseboat is history. Tony gave me the play to read and I was bowled over. I said to John when I met him that it would be compared to the novels of Kingsley Amis and John Wain, but what was remarkable was the use of contemporary language in theatrical rhetoric, like an Elizabethan play. With that play the efforts of T. S. Eliot and Christopher Fry to revive the blank-verse form and of Saint-Denis to rediscover a classic style became meaningless. At last there was a writer who had something to say and was writing for the theatre.

Tony invited me to supper with Osborne before the play was produced. The supper was cooked by Tony's flatmate, the

American sociologist George Goetschius – spaghetti and meat balls. I guess our image of John was of a rather macho figure, living on a barge. He arrived immaculate in blazer and bow-tie accompanied by Tony Creighton, his friend and co-author of *Epitaph for George Dillon*, a small camp figure dressed in a kilt. They announced they were vegetarians. There were whispered consultations in the kitchen. 'Do you think they're queer? What are we going to do with the meat balls?' I forget what they eventually ate but the dinner went off well. Apart from the little old lady from Hove it was my first experience of a living writer.

I wasn't part of that first season; I was still working for Granada TV (who did a memorable transmission of *Look Back*), but I saw nearly all the plays, usually at the preview or public dress rehearsal as it was called. Percy (Margaret) Harris, Sophie's sister and the other half of Motley, created a permanent surround in three sections; a curved cloth at the back and two side pieces in the form of 'a soft S' – in the words of Michael Halifax, the first stage director. The cloth was covered in net in the manner of the Berliner Ensemble. The first play, Angus Wilson's *The Mulberry Bush*, an interesting but conventional play of ideas, sat uneasily in the middle of this Brechtian surround. There was the simple unit of the door, that George had described in Berlin, but there was also a window and another door. Apart from the fact that they were not linked by walls we were in a box set. The second act had a huge mulberry tree in the middle of the stage. The play cried out for conventional treatment and no way could George or anyone else turn it into an epic piece. *The Crucible* which followed was better; a floor of bare boards and a massive wooden-frame ceiling-piece suspended on chains, designed by Stephen Doncaster. There was the Brechtian aesthetic if not the politics: they cut the part of Giles Corey, the one character who gives the play its economic and political perspective. There was a 'permanent' company but it already had visiting stars like Gwen Ffrangcon-Davies and Joan Greenwood. None the less it was the first real ensemble in Britain in which there were overall principles of design and staging, a group of actors and directors and a policy of new work. Even in the days of Granville-Barker each play had been cast separately.

Nineteen fifty-six was also the year in which Brecht died and the Berliner Ensemble came to London and changed my life. The first production we saw was *The Caucasian Chalk Circle* which was impressive and very beautiful to look at. In the interval I met John Dexter for the first time. He was already working at the Court. But it was *Courage* that blew our minds. When the half-curtain whizzed back and we saw Helene Weigel smiling up at the sky, Angelika Hurwicz blowing into her harmonica and the cart pulled against the revolve by a sweaty, piggy-eyed Ekkehard Schall and tiny, timid Heinz Schubert we knew this was it. They seemed to affront the audience in the Palace Theatre with their sureness. Nothing was hidden, nothing secret. It looked wonderful. They sang the song and the curtains shot together. End of scene one. The third play was *Trumpets and Drums*, the adaptation of *The Recruiting Officer*, which was again brilliantly designed by Karl von Appen, but had traces of campery that we didn't altogether like. But the actors, what actors! Earthy and funny and savage and tragic, we'd never seen anything like it.

The Court was in the middle of its first season and already the Brechtian design was proving difficult. The permanent surround was on its way out; the pieces of flown scenery kept catching in the net and Tony was moving towards more decorative staging and more exotic designers. Later Jocelyn Herbert, at that time the Court's scene-painter, resigned in protest at this trend. The failure of George's production of *The*

*Good Woman of Setzuan* with Peggy Ashcroft (Theo Otto had recreated his original sets on the much smaller Court stage) and the success of *The Country Wife* interrupted the Brechtian influence in Sloane Square. But some writers had been affected. *The Entertainer*, for all Osborne's disclaimers, used a freer theatre form than any he had used before and writers like John Arden were consciously absorbing the lessons of the Ensemble. Design could never quite be the same again and I knew I had to rethink everything.

The second season saw the development of George's plan for the future: the 'productions-without-décor', single Sunday night performances of new plays. These felt as historically important as anything in the main bill; the actors were paid expenses (Rita Webb, the Cockney actress who appeared in my Sunday night, was amazed to receive her two guineas: 'Blimey, I didn't expect money. I thought you was a load of bleeding amachoors') and the writers gave up all their rights for a fee of five pounds. Among the first productions were Lindsay Anderson's of *The Waiting of Lester Abbs* and John Dexter's of *Yes – and After* by Michael Hastings. I think I was number five. Tony gave me a play by N. F. Simpson, *A Resounding Tinkle*, which was one of the prize-winners in the *Observer* competition. I didn't really understand it but it was my only chance of breaking into the theatre where I, or anyone else of my generation, wanted to work.

The play in its original two-act form was a free-wheeling dissertation on the nature of comedy, with scenes from a play about Bro and Middie Paradock interspersed with meetings of the critics and two comedians attempting to test theories of laughter. Bro and Middie are a surburban couple who have bought an elephant, which is outside in their garden. They are dissatisfied with it, but even more with their failure to agree on a name for it. From time to time the doorbell goes. 'There's a man at the door. He wants you to form a government .' Later Uncle Ted turns up. 'Oh, Uncle Ted, you've changed your sex.' After *Monty Python* it sounds quite normal, but then its only ancestors were *Alice in Wonderland* and the Goon Show.

Here's some of the dialogue of the comedians:

A: Not that there's anything wrong with silence as far as that goes. It isn't so easily come by these days.

B: But it isn't what you go to the theatre for. That's all. You might go to some places for silence, but not a theatre. They'll feel cheated.

A: Tell me something. When you go into a shop and buy a bath sponge, and you find that the bath sponge is full of holes, and that something like two-thirds of what you've paid good money for isn't really there at all – do you feel you've been cheated?

B: It isn't the same thing.

A: Never mind. Do you feel cheated? Do you feel every time you buy a bath sponge which is made up of two-thirds holes that you're being overcharged? Because you are. You're being overcharged 200 per cent.

B: A sponge is where you expect to find holes. You buy it for the holes. But a theatre is not where you expect to find silence. That's the difference.

Simpson (known as Wally after the Duchess of Windsor) turned out to be a gaunt, grave man in his thirties who taught in a day college. I suspect the play had been boiling up in him for a long time. It was witty, imaginative, inventive and difficult. I cast it with actors like Nigel Davenport (a Court actor from the beginning) and Wendy Craig ( a discovery of Tony Richardson) as the Paradocks; Graham Crowden and Toke Townley as the comedians. Nothing of the little craft I'd acquired in weekly rep seemed relevant to the work; even less the dream I had of Stanislavsky-based production, objectives, beats and through lines and as for Brecht . . . Everything in the play worked against the schematic and the methodical. I was left with the authority of the text, its punctuation and, above all, its clearly marked pauses. Many of them seemed nonsensical, but were part of Wally's deeply felt beliefs about comedy. 'Wait longer,' he would say in rehearsal (just as Ralph Lynn would whisper to his partner, 'Don't say it yet, don't say it yet, say it . . . Now.'). For the first time in my life I was working with a writer, a live writer, who had no theatre background, was experimenting with dramatic form and knew how to do it.

The play was rehearsed in two weeks in the Parish Hall in Pavilion Road, where we rehearsed all the Court plays at that time. Both George and Tony were in America. George was reproducing *The Country Wife* on Broadway, but he flew back just in time to catch the performance on Sunday, 8 December 1957. Within minutes of the start of the play Wally was proved right; the pauses worked; the audience laughed. The actors were as amazed as I was.

The next morning George offered me a job as an Assistant to the Artistic Director and Oscar Lewenstein, then the General Manager, offered me a salary of fifteen pounds, exactly half what I'd been earning at Granada Television. I accepted gladly.

# 3

# The Stage Space

Directing in weekly rep was easy. The vast majority of plays were three-act, one-set plays, usually in domestic interiors of different levels of the middle class. The entrances were dictated by the kitchen, the dining room (if it was upper middle) and the outside. Everything on the stage was governed by the specific needs of the action of the play. The furniture was to permit conversation and there was always a sofa, usually at right-angles to the fire, facing front. Sometimes very daringly the fire would be imagined in the footlights to validate the position of the sofa but this meant that once the actors were settled on it it was impossible to motivate moves away to the mantelpiece so that you could lean on it, back to your fellow actor and emote into the fire. Everyone smoked and there were ashtrays on every available occasional table, containing water to eliminate fire risks. The similarity of the plays made it possible to rehearse them in a week, in a style of writing and acting that was constant. Design was a matter of using the same flats, cleated together in different formations and painted differently each week. The great art was 'dressing' the set – that is choosing the properties which were borrowed, on the promise of free seats, from shops in the town. If a china vase was broken the shop that loaned it would be out for all future borrowing. A new stage manager might arrive in a town to find all the shops closed to him. The fascination for me was to discover how far you could create verismo in the detail of the production in the space of a week. The discipline in the use of time was valuable too but could lead to short-cuts.

The alternative was Shakespeare, if you made it to Stratford or the Old Vic, which fortunately I didn't till after I had worked on new plays at the Royal Court. Production style, at that time, was still very pictorial, dominated by painters like Leslie Hurry, but tempered by elements of the Elizabethan playhouse transposed to the proscenium stage. Guthrie was the principal exponent of this kind of theatre and later took it to the extremes of the thrust or apron stage ('thrust' if you can imagine it advancing sexually into the middle of the audience, 'apron' if you see it spreading out sideways) in the theatres he built in Stratford, Ontario and at Minneapolis. Some modification of his concept is seen at the Olivier and Barbican theatres. The hallmark of Guthrie's style was constant movement. He was a restless director on the proscenium stage but on the thrust stage movement was essential if all the audience were to see the actors' faces, at least some of the time. In those days the great crime was to stand still and a director was judged by his ability to move his actors round the stage, which Guthrie did brilliantly.

My love affair with the French theatre had made me understand that there was an alternative to endless movement. In my production of *George Dandin* the actors, in modern dress, sat on the stage all the time and got up for their entrances. I already knew that 'less was more'. Étienne Decroux, who taught me mime, used to quote Victor Hugo: 'Rien est plus émouvant qu'une statue qui présente la mobilité.' In Vilar's work at the TNP the simplicity of staging was unlike anything to be seen in London and with the work of the Berliner Ensemble it was at last clear how a production could be simple, apparently static and yet wholly dynamic. When Mother Courage pulls her cart against the movement of the revolving stage she is, in fact, static but thinks she is moving forwards, using all her effort to stay in the same place, a visual presentation of the small business woman in a competitive world. When I came to work on Brecht's plays I started to realize the exact political significance of each stage picture and the movement between one static picture and the next. The model books in which the productions of the Berliner Ensemble are recorded are, in some sense, like the storyboard of a film. Each moment is meaningful – in their work politically meaningful – and the movement from one picture to the next must indicate change. It's a theory that can never work on Guthrie's open stages where there is no fixed viewpoint shared by the whole audience.

Brecht's Epic Theatre is both aesthetic and didactic. Aesthetic because it makes beautiful pictures, didactic because the dramatist/director makes the audience focus on what will be instructive, moving his pointer round the stage like a school-teacher on a blackboard. Actors can move dynamically back-wards and forwards but their placing is seen laterally across the stage. The division of the stage, left and right, becomes important. In the old theatre the leading actor occupied the centre of the stage, the so-called point of command. He is Hamlet advancing down the middle to tell us his inner thoughts, or Lear dividing his kingdom on a throne that divides the stage. From left and right we focus on the centre and empathize with the hero. With Brecht no one is so important that he may occupy the centre line. Often Brecht divides the stage in contrasting groups which make a dialectic when seen together. Courage discusses the progress of the war behind the wagon while Kattrin dresses up in the whore's red boots in front of it; Galileo and his pupils make experiments that disprove Aristotle in one half of the stage, while his daughter and the housekeeper chatter about horoscopes in the other. This is a demonstration of thesis, antithesis and synthesis with the audience synthesizing from the contrasting scenes they watch.

Although I have never believed that the purpose of theatre is only political, it was from an understanding of the political intent of Brecht's staging that I saw that it was the director's job to maintain the objective control of the stage picture and its meaning. It was clear that for this to work there must be no unnecessary clobber on the stage, no Cecil Beaton flower arrangements, no Leslie Hurry backdrops, no Oliver Messel gauzes. The human figure must exist in space with only such elements of architecture and physical properties as were absolutely necessary. Perhaps this also chimes with that part of English good taste which is puritanical. But it is not just a spartan aesthetic. It is concerned with keeping a sense of what the play is about, what it is trying to say, whether didactically or not. It was a lesson that I started to learn in 1956. The most usual approving comment on my work is that 'it's so clear'. What do they expect it to be. Muddy?

About the same time I came under the influence of Yat Malmgren, the movement teacher, who taught me something of Rudolph von Laban's theory of space. Like Brecht's his theory is based on the proscenium theatre. The theatre is a three-dimensional space with height, width and depth in which the actor moves forwards and backwards, left and right and on the diagonals. The diagonals are the longest distance an actor can travel in a straight line. Yat taught me how the directions of movement on the stage in themselves create dramatic effects; to enter upstage centre and move straight down the centre line is dominating and purposeful, to enter at one of the upstage corners and cross downstage to the opposite corner is more thoughtful. If you have downstage exits, as there are at the Royal Court, the diagonal move has an extension beyond the stage space into the imaginary world offstage. When I came to work at the Court this concept of the space began to be felt in the design. There is little wing space and the simplest use of the stage area is to have two upstage entrances at the corners of a box-like surround matched by the two downstage entrances in what are laughingly called the assemblies. (Our first stage director came from Stratford-upon-Avon where spear carriers used to assemble for processions. You were lucky if you could assemble a paper bag in our proscenium entrances.) In fact they were two former stage boxes which had been converted into entrances when the forestage was added. In my production of *Macbeth* Duncan's chamber was downstage left. When Macduff emerged from discovering the murder he ran to each of the other exits as he shouted, 'Horror, horror, horror' offstage. It was a simple way of creating the space outside the visible space of the stage. Again, the Court stage is narrow but reasonably deep for its width. Lady Macbeth enters for the sleep-walking scene and is talked about by the Doctor and the Gentlewoman for some time before she starts speaking. This was no problem on the wide Elizabethan stage but difficult at the Court. The only solution was to bring her on upstage and travel straight ahead turning at right-angles at each corner of the box. The dance critic David Vaughan said it was like the sleep walker in Balanchine's ballet *Night Shadow* and certainly the use of space owes something to the dance world. But once you understand the basic concept the placing of scenery and properties inside the space becomes more significant.

The other dimension of the stage is height. The Court has a high proscenium in relation to its width and because of its lack of wing space one has to rely on flying scenic elements within the space. After Brecht it became a standard and often rather boring practice to have a section of a wall flown in to indicate a room. Since Brecht, plays that demand frequent changes of locale have become the rule rather than the exception. 'Away with the Aristotelian unities. We want Epic Theatre showing the full range of society.' I'm afraid this has become an excuse for lazy writers – who can't be bothered with the disciplines of theatre and would really rather write for films and television – to set any scene where they like, indoors or outdoors, forgetting, though it is the easiest thing in the world to indicate change of place by a single flat or even a slide projection, that you can't simultaneously bring a dining-room suite or a whole café with tables and chairs on to the stage, particularly as there is no room for them in the wings. To change scenery is never a problem; to change furniture is a major headache.

The stage at the Court also had its original 'grave' trap (for Ophelia) and its two 'star' traps (star because they were originally star-shaped and could be pushed up by the head of the actor and close behind him). In pantomime they were always used by the Fairy Queen (stage right) and the Demon King (stage left). The addition of the forestage had placed the grave trap too far upstage so a new rectangular trap was made downstage centre, though without the extensive mechanism of the grave trap. The traps were also used to provide scenic elements which could quickly be got rid of. The offstage areas of an old theatre have a kind of mystery because they exist as a living part of theatre beyond what the audience sees, outside that empty space in which the action happens. This was one of the revelations of the Moscow Art Theatre on its visit to London in 1957, the sense of actors entering from a distance, coming from somewhere, and the amazing sound effects. When I came to rehearse *Three Sisters* at the Court I spent hours trying to emulate their offstage fire-engine and crowd noises. Eventually I ended up under the stage directing an improvisation with all the members of the company who were not in the scene. Suddenly I had a sensation of the community of theatre, all of us struggling, out of sight, to create something for the box of light above us and an awareness of the theatre stretching above and below that space, a space that Beckett thought should have the maximum of corporal and verbal presence.

It's perhaps significant that the contemporary work of the English Stage Company should have thrived in an old-fashioned proscenium theatre. The austere work of the Berliner Ensemble, too, was shown behind a proscenium of gilt cupids at the Theater am Schiffbauerdamm, a theatre about which Brecht and Weigel were quite sentimental. George Devine had a great love of the traditional crafts of theatre. It stopped the work being trendy and gave a focus to the new plays that they would not otherwise have had.

# 4

# Joining the Court;
## *George Dillon*
## and New York

When I joined the staff at the Court the only other Assistant to
the Artistic Director, or AAD, was John Dexter, whose Sunday night production I'd admired. Later we were joined by
Lindsay Anderson, and then by Antony Page. Dexter had
come to the Court through John Osborne, whom he'd known
in rep at Derby when John was writing – or at least living –
*Look Back in Anger.* He was rumoured to be the original of
Webster, 'the female Emily Brontë' in Osborne's play. Anyway I liked him. He'd been an actor in *The Archers* and a stage
manager in rep and we got on immediately. Although George
Devine would have been horrified if he'd realized it, most of
his directors were homosexual, ranging from closet queen and
bisexual to the fairly blatant Dexter and myself. Soon after I'd
settled in as an AAD John was given the sack after we'd been
found cuddling in our little office. 'We think he's a bad
influence on you, Bill,' said Tony Richardson. However, John
was soon back after the success of his Wesker productions at
Coventry. He was working class and had none of the educa-
tional background of the rest of us, which isolated him.
George, Tony and Lindsay had all been at Wadham College,
Oxford; Tony Page and I were both Oxford men too. I was
closer to John because my background was provincial petit-
bourgeois whereas Lindsay and Tony Page had both been born
in Bangalore, the sons of army officers, and had been brought

up by ayahs. Having a nanny is as big a class divide as any. The ethics of the forces and public school were always in evidence.

Dexter and I shared a windowless office by the upper circle, which became the port of call for all writers; there was no literary manager (Ken Tynan imported the European idea of the *Dramaturg* in 1963) but there was a tradition of giving writers work by getting them to read scripts at five shillings a time. Osborne had been a prolific script-reader till he became a success. Edward Bond was to become the Court's star reader but the supervision of the reading was in the hands of Keith Johnstone, a large earnest man who chewed huge cooking apples and carried his scripts around in carrier bags. When he met me he said he was pleased to meet someone even more nervous than he was. He'd come to the Court through Lindsay Anderson and had collaborated on an early Free Cinema film script and had no previous connection with theatre. In consequence his judgements were raw and penetrating. John Arden called him 'the unpaid conscience of the Royal Court'. George and Tony ignored most of his advice, but listened to what he said.

In those days the theatre was hardly ever dark. It was thought highly uncommercial to allow this to happen. After the last night of a production the set was struck and the new set put up and lit. The technical rehearsal would last most of the night. The actors would come in on Sunday to rehearse, there would be a preview on Monday and the show would open to the critics on Tuesday. The front curtain, a tatty set of crumpled plum velvet , was nearly always used. A wheezy old recording of the National Anthem would start the evening; this was standard practice but much resented by anti-monarchists. Many people thought the Court was being deliberately disrespectful by using this scratched record. There was no legal reason to use it and later it was dropped entirely for the first night of *Look After Lulu*, the Court's most untypical piece of commercial theatre (Vivien Leigh, Noël Coward and Binkie Beaumont), and has never reappeared since. The lighting was in the hands of the director. There were no prima-donna lighting designers, which usually meant it ended up in George's capable hands.

I had been an AAD only a week when George offered me the first professional production of *Epitaph for George Dillon*, an early play by Osborne, which he had written with his friend in the kilt, Tony Creighton. I guess Tony Richardson didn't want to direct it. *Look Back* had been a huge success on Broadway; *The Entertainer* rather less so, but Tony was already involved with other American plans and film projects. I loved the play, which is about the eruption of Dillon, an actor and writer, into a lower-middle-class family. It is conventional in form but has a stunning duologue in the second act between George and Ruth, the unmarried, left-wing aunt of the family – the only example in Osborne's work of a major scene between a man and a woman. It was also about an actor in digs in the provinces and his search for work, which I knew pretty well.

The play was to be part of a season in repertoire. Ann Jellicoe, another *Observer* prize-winner, was to direct her own play *The Sport of My Mad Mother*. Ann had been an actress and run her own theatre. She is warm, breezy and sometimes bossy. Like Keith Johnstone she has poor eyesight and large spectacles. For a time they were very influenced by Aldous Huxley's *The Art of Seeing* and went round wearing eyepatches on alternate eyes. *Sport*, as her play was soon known, is a remarkable piece, even more remarkable in 1958; a strange projection of the lives of teenagers in an urban desert, written in compressed, rhythmic dialogue. Its only ancestor is Eliot's *Sweeney Agonistes*. Ann and I had to form a company based on the two plays; the third was still undecided. This was the first time I had been able to cast a play from the full range of London actors. Robert Stephens was to play George Dillon; he had been with the Court from the beginning but this was to be his first leading part. I offered the part of Ruth to two actresses, both of whom accepted, and George had to sort out the mess, pleading my inexperience. It was eventually played by Yvonne Mitchell. The rest of the company was Wendy Craig, Nigel Davenport and Toke Townley from my Sunday production, Alison Leggatt, a character actress who had worked with Noël Coward, Avril Elgar, Philip Locke and Paul Bailey, who later became a novelist. Harold Pinter, with whom I'd kept in contact, was the understudy.

This was the first time I had rehearsed a play for more than two weeks. Although I shared a cast with Ann, three of my principals were not in *Sport*. Carefully I divided the play into units and objectives as laid down by Stanislavsky. The set by Stephen Doncaster was a realistic living room but placed at an angle to the proscenium so that the room had two fourth walls instead of one. Inside the room the furniture was arranged exactly as I remembered it from my time in digs: on one wall the fire with the sofa facing it, a bay window on the other. You could see the front door from outside, the hall, the stairs and the kitchen beyond the living room. The play in its original form had three flashbacks, one in each act, and these were played on a cantilevered platform over the main playing area. One corner of the room projected on to the forestage and contained the table with the picture of the son killed in the First World War, surrounded by Flanders poppies. The last line of Act One was Bob Stephens picking it up and saying, 'You stupid-looking bastard.' His other great moment was in the last act when he has become a successful writer of cheap plays and is given a present by the family. It's wrapped in stiff brown paper and Bob asks archly, 'What have we heah?' as he unwraps it. It is a typewriter. Bob held one of those endless pauses during which the audience thinks as one with him, 'the present will be trite and unimaginative', then 'it's sensitive and appropriate', and then bitterly 'but now it's going to be used to write rubbish on'.

The play was written before *Look Back in Anger* and though George, in some ways, is an early sketch for Jimmy Porter the play is more of an ensemble piece than anything Osborne wrote later and the cast played it with all the humour and sensibility of the best British character acting. The Moscow Art Theatre had followed the Berliner Ensemble to London and, though not as far reaching in their influence, had been much admired. Yosef Rayevski, the director of *Three Sisters* wrote a warm appreciation of our work in *Encore* magazine. Later, in New York, Noël Coward came to see the play and said, 'Of course, we are wonderful at ensemble acting. That's why the Americans admire you so much. They can't do it.'

*Dillon* was not a huge hit but it did transfer to the West End. Donald Albery thought the title gloomy and wanted us to change it to *Telephone Tart* (the title suggested for Dillon's soft-porn touring show by Barney Evans, 'the poor man's Binkie'). Albery eventually called it just *George Dillon*. When it transferred to Broadway, produced by David Merrick and Josh Logan, the Americans referred to it as *Epitaph*. Most of the British cast were in the Broadway production – this was before both unions were strict. Eileen Herlie replaced Yvonne Mitchell and Frank Finlay made his début as the father. Every single prop was lovingly packed and sent from Britain by Michael Halifax, our stage director, with details of the place settings for the different meals. Above all, the cocktail cabinet that lit up – 'You'd never find a bad-taste object like that over here,' Josh Logan said.

We opened in Baltimore and then went on to Atlantic City, where we played in a 3000-seat picture palace of the thirties, designed like an Italian Renaissance city with cypress trees and copies of Michelangelo's *David* in niches. Our little Royal Court set from a proscenium opening twenty-one-foot wide sat in a huge expanse of blackness more than three times its width. From the back it looked like a small TV set. When the play started the ceiling and half the walls were transformed into a Mediterranean night sky with stars twinkling in it. They were surprised when we asked them to turn off the effects.

We opened in New York at the John Golden Theater, one of the few Broadway houses of comparable size to the Royal Court. The play was well received at the end and we trooped off to a vast party at Josh Logan's. I think most of the party were the British contingent, but they certainly counted as foreigners to us. The play was particularly liked in New York – perhaps for the very reason it was received coolly in London – because it was about the uncertainty of being an actor and the struggle between integrity and compromise. At the end George Dillon has compromised but he is a SUCCESS. Josh greeted us at the party like heroes. 'The show is a hit,' he announced. 'I thought you could never say that in New York till the notices came out,' I ventured. 'Look, young man,' he roared, 'when I say a show is a hit, it's a hit.' I went off to have a drink with the company. Not long after it was noticeable that the room was emptying or rather that there was a mad rush to the door like water running out of a bath. The notices had arrived. I went over to Josh and said in effect, 'I told you so', perhaps not the most tactful thing in the circumstances. 'I knew there was something wrong with the third act. You should have done something about it.' 'Why the fuck didn't you say that before?' I wasn't exactly thrown out but I did hit Walter Winchell's column the next morning. I wandered round the bars of New York and eventually phoned George Devine and told him the news. 'Don't worry, boy,' he said. 'There's plenty of work back here.' I knew then that I was secure, not in the certainty of a regular job but in the values of Devine and the theatre he ran. The hysteria and panic and glamour of Broadway were light-years away from the work in which we were involved.

There was an interesting coda to the story of *Dillon*, which shows the other, warm, sentimental side of Broadway. Although the show was a flop because of the notices, it had a passionate minority following. People, usually theatre people, would weep in the streets after the performance. We were, that unknown thing in New York, a flop *d'estime*. One night Coward came to see it with Marlene Dietrich. They came round afterwards and we told them we were closing at the end of the week. 'Von meenit,' Marlene said. 'Zees play is put on by Meester Merrick, ees it not?' We said it was. 'I go to see him now.' By coincidence she was having supper with Merrick and some of his backers at Sardi's to discuss her appearance in a musical version of her great film hit *Destry Rides Again*. She swept into Sardi's and refused to discuss the project until she had forced Merrick and the angels to guarantee a further week's run of the play. Not content she went off to find Bob Stephens and Eileen Herlie, who, by this time, had gone on to a party for another show which was a real HIT, to tell them the news. It ran for only that extra week but it was revived on Broadway in the same season, a thing unprecedented in Broadway history, because of a pressure group led by Coward, Dietrich and Tennessee Williams.

# 5

# The Writers' Group

In less than a year I'd been whisked from a Sunday night to a main-bill production that transferred to the West End, shot across the Atlantic and been fought for by mythical figures like Coward and Dietrich. Even though the values of Broadway were transparently hollow they were in some way related to the way the Court was run. Without a very good percentage deal from David Merrick over the transfer of the Osborne plays the operation in Sloane Square could not have survived, least of all on its pathetically small Arts Council grant. And in spite of George's promise of 'plenty of work' there was not really enough to keep Anderson, Dexter and myself occupied. Even after the flop of *Dillon* I was offered more work on Broadway and because there was nothing to do in Sloane Square I accepted. I lived through the agony of the rehearsals, the opening in Philadelphia or Newhaven, the rewrites, the replacements, the hysterical pressures by the producer, which have been so often recorded. On one show, *Moonbirds*, a fey comedy by Marcel Aymé, which opened in Philadelphia to disastrous notices, I was replaced after a week of misery in which I lost a stone in weight. When the show finally opened in New York it ran two nights. People thought I was quite smart to get out of such a turkey.

Half of me was caught up in the glamour and excitement of it all, the other half was still dreaming of ensemble theatre and what we were going to do to change things back home. *Dillon* was followed in the repertoire by Ann Jellicoe's *The Sport of My Mad Mother*, which was supposed to be directed by Ann and George, but though George oversaw the staging it was in every important aspect directed by Ann. It was the first of the really experimental plays to be done in the main bill. None of us knew what to make of it – a play about Teds and their girls in a pattern of rhythmic one-line dialogue – but we were very excited by the way it was opening up the language and imagery of theatre. It had some exciting performances: Philip Locke as a Ted in bubble wig and beetle crushers, ageless Avril Elgar as the waif Dodo, and Sheila Ballantine in a rhythmic sequence called 'the perming of Pattie', which was the instructions on the back of a home permanent wave chanted by the group.

The play was designed by Jocelyn Herbert, the first of her classically simple sets: a billboard of gleaming anodized zinc, a solitary pylon or lamp surrounded by darkness. We were all gathered at the dress rehearsal, Ann and George, Jocelyn, Dexter, Keith Johnstone and myself. Something was wrong. The set looked too pure, too clinical; it had no feel of people's lives. Keith went away and came back with a group of working-class kids he was teaching and gave them chalks to draw with. In the middle of the technical rehearsal the kids solemnly drew on the shining metal giving it some kind of context and humanity. The rehearsal went on.

We were all mad about the play and half hoped it would be a success in the way the Osborne plays had been. We even stayed up to read the notices, which, apart from Ken Tynan's, were foul. It was taken off at the end of its second week and replaced in the repertoire by *Dillon*, which was doing moderately well. This commercial ruthlessness was part of the pattern of the Court's existence at that time. No one knew from one year to the next whether the organization would survive. It was not unlike Broadway. If a show got bad notices its life was limited and there was so little advance booking that it could be taken off and something else substituted at a moment's notice, usually at the instigation of the Chairman of the Council, Neville Blond. He even wanted us to keep five actors permanently on salary ready to do *Look Back in Anger*, our sure breadwinner, whenever anything flopped. But every night of the run of *Sport of My Mad Mother* there was a group of writers and directors cheering and stamping at the back of an almost empty house. It was the beginning of the embattled community which provided the creative core of the work over the next few years. Keith Johnstone went to every performance and began a relationship with Ann, sexual as well as artistic, which was to influence both their lives.

The next play was to have been the first English production of *Endgame* but it was in trouble with the Lord Chamberlain over one line, 'The swine he doesn't exist', which Beckett refused to change. Something else had to be found and quickly. Wally Simpson had reduced the Bro and Middie section of *A Resounding Tinkle* to a one-act play and very quickly wrote a companion piece, *The Hole*, his most brilliant and anti-philosophical piece of work. There is a hole in the road and a group of individuals, who are named after their psychological types (Cerebro, Endo, etc.) peer into it and see different things. It sounds very dusty and quaint. In fact it released all the highest flights of Wally's comic fantasy. Two men meet warmly. 'Harry,' 'I remember your name as if it were yesterday – but I'm damned if I haven't completely forgotten your face for a moment.' 'Let me show you a photograph.' In the company were Wendy Craig and Nigel Davenport from the original *Tinkle* and

*The Hole* was easily cast from the resident company. The show opened just before Easter 1958. On Good Friday we set off on the first Aldermaston March.

There was a real feeling of change and excitement in the air. The work at the Court had opened the door to writers whose political involvement was certainly greater than the founders of the English Stage Company or most of us working there: writers like Christopher Logue and Doris Lessing who were politically committed but not primarily theatre people like Osborne or Pinter. In the most reactionary branch of the arts – the theatre – the new work was reflecting, if not producing, social change. It was inevitable that we were all swept up in a pacifist, idealistic movement like the Campaign for Nuclear Disarmament though demonstrating was a new experience for us. Jocelyn Herbert seemed most at home, but then she'd marched in the thirties. We went along on that first Good Friday because it was the thing to do. Lindsay Anderson was filming us and there's a shot of me in the film with Lessing, Logue and, I think, John Berger sitting on the grass at Turnham Green. Harold Pinter watched us from his flat in the Chiswick High Road but didn't join the march. 'William Shakespeare, William Blake, we are marching for your sake,' we chanted.

On the second day it rained and some of us turned back. Among those who were going to go all the way was a young couple, bright-eyed and rosy-cheeked, the embodiment of good health and idealism – Arnold and Dusty Wesker. Lindsay had already read and been encouraging about Arnold's first play and on the march Dexter met Wesker. They started talking in a church hall in Slough with the rain pouring down outside. It was a dialogue that led to a series of wonderful productions over the next three years. I got back from the march on Easter Monday to find that Tynan's notice in the

*Observer* the day before had filled the theatre for the Simpson double-bill.

Within a matter of months a group of writers and directors had come together in Sloane Square, under the wing of George Devine but separate from the globe-trotting stars Osborne and Richardson. We were the second wave. Ann Jellicoe and Keith Johnstone found they shared many basic attitudes with Wally Simpson and Harold Pinter. They tried to formulate these in a letter to *The Times* in which they declared their belief in theatre as a demonstration through images, in which words expressed relationships but were never used for the promotion or discussion of ideas. They hated Shaw and all he stood for. They were moral rather than political, but I think Harold and Wally drew back from all committed attitudes, just as they drew back from narrative. No morality without narrative. Wally once said he was frightened of being disloyal to chaos. I sat in on their debate and wondered how this related to the Brechtian theory I half understood, in which narrative was the crucial element.

Pinter never became a Royal Court writer, though *The Room* and *The Dumb Waiter* were later transferred there from Hampstead. I had shown George both these plays after they were first done in Bristol, but Harold Hobson in his notice in *The Sunday Times* had said that they should be done at the Court and George hated to be told what to do by a critic. It was a pity because in some ways George was more sympathetic to politically uncommitted writers like Simpson and Pinter than to Arnold Wesker, whose first produced play, *Chicken Soup with Barley*, was directed by Dexter at Coventry that summer. John Arden had arrived on the scene too, but his political commitment was more acceptable to Devine because of his songs and his poetic language.

Any writer whom the Court wished to encourage was given a pass, which enabled them to see productions free, watch

rehearsals and come to the meetings that George would have
from time to time in his house in Hammersmith or in the
workshop in Park Street at the end of the King's Road. These
usually drifted into theoretical discussion. In one of my unem-
ployed periods I suggested to George that we should meet
regularly and I would be responsible for whatever happened.
Ann Piper, the novelist, who had written a play that had been
liked but not enough for it to be performed, was one of the
writers and she offered her house on the river, two doors from
the Devine house, as the meeting place. She had a large room
on the first floor which always had a blazing fire and there was
fresh coffee and bread and cheese for the hungry writers.
Neither Simpson nor Pinter joined the group though we were
still close friends. It smacked too much of Ionesco's description of Brecht, 'un théâtre de boy-scout'.

The only idea in my head when I started the group was that
we would not discuss each other's work or read passages from
it. The class would be an acting class in which everyone would
take part. We would learn what we wanted to find out about
theatre by doing it. The first class began with an exercise from
my mime teacher, Étienne Decroux, in which you place a
single chair in the centre of the space as the basis of improvisation. This has become the basis of so many exercises since and
perhaps fed into Edward Bond's mind for the last scene of
*Saved*. Bond was a quiet serious little man who followed
everything intently and improvised not particularly well but
with great concentration. He had been invited to join the
group because of a play he had submitted called *Klaxon in
Atreus Palace* which I couldn't understand at all, but Keith had
liked. With hindsight I suppose its title implied 'I am going to
show these ancient Greeks what a working-class writer can
do.' There were others too – Maureen Duffy, who soon
decided that the novel was her medium – and occasionally

Edna O'Brien. The stalwarts were Jellicoe and Johnstone, Arden, Wesker, Bond and Wole Soyinka. Soyinka's chair improvisation was of being cruised in the cinema.

We moved on to Stanislavsky improvisations on objectives. I sent Donald Howarth to borrow money from Ann Piper who was preparing the bread and cheese in the kitchen. Of course he succeeded. Later we started to probe what Brecht was all about by reading *Der Jasager* and *Der Neinsager* and improvising on the basis of using only statement and question. On a never-to-be-forgotten occasion George showed us the use of comic masks. Keith describes this well in his book *Impro*.

George may have thought the class went badly but Keith was seized with excitement. So was I, and John Arden wrote his play *The Happy Haven*, which I directed at the Court in 1960, especially for masks. Very occasionally we would improvise on a scene if a writer was stuck. Ann Jellicoe brought us an idea from the play she was writing. We were playing round an old bed. Bored with the way it was going – I was in the impro – I said, 'It's not a bed, it's a piano.' 'It's a bed,' insisted Harriet Devine (about sixteen at the time) and we were off, to be immortalized in *The Knack*.

One of the pieces of work that evolved from the group was *Eleven Men Dead at Hola Camp*. Eleven detainees had been beaten to death in Kenya and Keith and I decided to stage a dramatized protest on a Sunday evening. We had never done anything as positively political as this before, nor had the Court, and the Council were shit-scared. There was a rule banning coverage of matters to be discussed in Parliament within a certain numbers of days; there was no script and we planned to have on-the-spot improvisation. From all points of view it was risky. The Council insisted we consulted Gerald Gardiner. Gardiner was surprisingly reassuring and the show went ahead. We got together a group of black actors and improvised on the material as it had appeared in the White Paper and on what we could find out about the Mau Mau. The group included Africans, West Indians and Britons who were united only by the colour of their skin. Bloke Modisane from South Africa would tell us how you had to put your face in the way of a blow from the police because marks on the body of a black man were not clear enough for a court of law. The Sunday evening was a strange mixture of inadequate improvisation, political passion, beautiful songs by Wole Soyinka, and tremendous audience response. It was way ahead of its time and came out of our group commitment.

The group held together for about three years, I suppose. CND grew and Wesker and I were invited by Bertrand Russell to become part of the Committee of 100, a group of well-known people committed to civil disobedience. We had moved on from peace marches to sit-downs. While planning one of these sit-downs half the committee, including Wesker, Robert Bolt and Christopher Logue were arrested. It was a predictably counter-productive move on the part of the government. Many people who would not have dreamt of it otherwise, like John Osborne, joined in the sit-down in Trafalgar Square. We knew the police were going to cordon off the square at some point and realized we would have to rendezvous somewhere till the time of the demonstration, which was fixed for three o'clock. I travelled by bus with John Arden. John, who always aped the gypsy in his dress, was for once wearing a suit as a form of disguise. I was wearing a rather camp striped mackintosh. 'You look very conspicuous,' John said. 'So do you,' I replied. We got off the bus and went into the cafeteria at the National Gallery. But everyone else had had the same idea; it was full of theatre people pretending not to know each other, rather like a Hitchcock film. When Big Ben struck three we swept out into the square. Everyone – but everyone, my dear – was there. Soon arrests were made. The word went round. 'They've got Vanessa.' I ended up in a cell with Lindsay, Antony Page, who had also joined the AADs, and Alan Sillitoe.

We were fined the next morning and were back at the Court by lunchtime. Wesker and the rest were released from prison and everything returned to normal. The Writers' Group ceased to function in spite of efforts to revive it. It had played an important part in all our lives. I had started to learn about teaching, which was to become very central to my work, and the writers had explored new approaches to theatre and, more important, had shared creative experiences with friends. To John Whiting and others outside the group it sounded pretentious and cliquey, but to us it was a warm and fertile time.

I think we knew we were the centre of the Court's work though all the writers were box-office risks. To begin with we thought every new play had the potential of an Osborne and might be magicked into the West End. Wesker's *Roots* with the support of Bernard Levin did have a brief run at the Duke of York's and Simpson's *One Way Pendulum*, which I directed in 1959, was a fashionable success and ran for some months at the Criterion. Wally and I had worked away at the structure of the play for nearly a year. His anarchic imagination is difficult to contain in the bounds of a full-length play and the comic ideas are so brilliant that they exhaust themselves quickly. Historically he is the link between the Goons and the zanier members of *Beyond the Fringe*. The play opened, as was traditional, at the Theatre Royal, Brighton, to the most conservative audience in the country. For the whole week there was not a single laugh; the actors were in despair and started to distrust the play and my direction. We came to the Court the following week and at the first preview the audience fell about. We were a sophisticated hit. It was the only starless success of that time.

But it was the exception rather than the rule. Writer after writer had been savaged by the critics. Arden fared the worst. After the first night of *Serjeant Musgrave's Dance* George arrived brandishing the notices, saying, with almost a note of triumph, 'They're even worse than *Live Like Pigs*.' Arden's next play was *The Happy Haven*, the product of the mask class, and it emptied the house. Its central characters were a group of old people, played by young actors – Susan Engel, Rachel Roberts and Frank Finlay – in masks. At the same time Noël Coward's *Waiting in the Wings*, a sentimental piece about ageing actors in a home, opened to acclaim in the West End. It was obvious we were not going to change the face of the commercial theatre. In 1958 Jellicoe, Pinter and Arden had all experienced ritual slaughter from the critics. Keith Johnstone hit back with a Sunday night play, *The Nigger Hunt*, in which the critics are personated as a terrible giant, wielding notices instead of a club, who is hunting a black writer. The writer escapes by painting his face white, an idea Wole Soyinka was to use in his play *The Invention*.

The rest of the programme at the Court was a mixed bag: classics like Shaw, Chekhov and Ibsen directed by George and plays set in the Deep South, like *Orpheus Descending*, or the West Indies, directed by Tony Richardson, which gave opportunities for elaborate stage designs by Loudon Sainthill. Often the three AADs had to fight for our own writers against the opposition of George and Tony and our last achievement as a group was to push through the Wesker Trilogy in 1960. Soon after, Anderson and I left. Dexter stayed until 1963 when he and I joined Olivier at the newly formed National Theatre.

# 6

# Improvisation
# and Text

A lot of my working life has been spent teaching. I've taught
when I couldn't find work as a director, when I was dissatisfied
with my directing and as a preparation for and during the
process of rehearsal. Glen Byam Shaw once said to me that
there was a greater sense of power in teaching than in directing
and it's true that when you teach you're up to your elbows in
the dough of the actor's creativity, not just steering him round
the furniture. Teaching has no time limit, whereas directing,
even with an extended rehearsal period, is governed by the
approach of the first night. In our time some of the very best
directors, such as Joan Littlewood and Peter Brook, have
thought it essential to use research into ways of acting as part of
their production process, though I think it is the professional
skill of both of them that enables them to pull a show together
in the last stages of rehearsal. I have often found the transition
from the research process to the putting of a show on the stage,
what the French so accurately call *mise-en-scène*, extremely
difficult. Perhaps a failure of nerve. But from Stanislavsky
onwards there has been a continual dissatisfaction with conventional acting methods and a recurring need to explore new
ways.

I have never adhered to a method of training actors, or even
tried to evolve one. There are basic approaches I use but they
are not part of a system. They have evolved over the years

from hints thrown out by practitioners, from absorbing the theories of Brecht and Stanislavsky and trying to relate them to practice – often very difficult. I must have read *An Actor Prepares* when I was very young without understanding it at all; it seemed stiff and pompous. It was only when I met the actor Harold Lang, who explained to me how the method worked and got me to read *Stanislavsky Directs*, which is not by the great man but by someone who actually recorded the day-to-day rehearsals, that I began to understand what it was all about. With Brecht it was easier because I had barely read any of the theory when I was overwhelmed by the experience of the practice. If the theory produced those results it was worth taking seriously.

All of us round the Court were constantly discussing these methods and their relevance to the work of new writers. There was also the Copeau–Saint-Denis tradition as handed on to us by George Devine, which was primarily concerned with new approaches to the text, particularly a classic text. It was not an approach that attempted to find new forms of theatre of the kind we were to see in the sixties, from which the writer was virtually excluded. However, George had used improvisation, mainly comic improvisation and mask work, in his teaching at the London Theatre Studio and later at the Vic School, and harboured a secret need to return to it. Tony Richardson was very scornful of this side of George and would say, 'We don't want any of that Saint-Denis rubbish in this theatre' at Council meetings, provoking outraged cries from Peggy Ashcroft, a passionate devotee of Saint-Denis. But this was to be the third big influence on my teaching and, to a lesser extent, my productions.

When we arrived for our first mask class the masks were already laid out on the table. We viewed them nervously while George talked, rather ponderously, about the tradition of the *commedia dell'arte*. Then he demonstrated how you choose a mask, study it, put it on and look in a mirror. When he turned round he was suddenly transformed into what Keith Johnstone called 'a toad god' who looked at us with contempt and snorted. It lasted probably less than a minute but it shook us. I understood in that moment that there was another approach to acting which was not analytical, in which the actor does not prepare in the Stanislavsky sense by thinking of the given circumstances, the 'flow of the day' or even his objectivity, but empties his mind to receive the influence, the identity, of another being. When you first see yourself in the mirror you see someone who is strange – you, but not you. In the moment of shock you respond, leave the mirror and try to move as your character. It helps to have a selection of simple props and costumes, hats, sticks, scarves, because these mask characters live on the sense of touch and in relation to material objects. Perhaps because of their limited vision they often appear grasping and possessive. The hat and a prop help to complete the character. The improvisation, sometimes solo, sometimes with another mask, usually last for a very short time. Because the assumption of character is so immediate it's difficult to sustain and the actor must take the mask off as soon as he feels his identity slipping. Any attempt to cheat or keep the improvisation going technically is apparent to everyone watching.

These masks were half-masks, with the actor's mouth and chin exposed. George called them comic or character masks as opposed to the classic full mask, with the mouth sealed off, that Copeau had also developed. These were used in tragic improvisations on simple fixed scenarios and there were only three kinds for each sex: young, middle-aged and old. I never really understood this neutral mask. Most of my work was with the comic masks that had been George Devine's speciality at the Old Vic School. The characters that emerge can be repeated and gradually learn to speak. They are invariably self-centred, childish, wilful and perverse. If you try to create a good or generous mask the character that emerges is usually silly and spineless. This may have something to do with the personality of the mask-maker. Every idiosyncrasy in the maker's character will transmit itself into the contours of the mask and consequently to the actor's performance. The Japanese say that the most difficult mask to make is that of the beautiful young girl, just because it must have no character and be perfectly smooth.

Masks became a central part of my teaching in those early years when I taught at a youth club in the Walworth Road as well as at drama schools and for the British Drama League. They work particularly well with amateurs and children; anyone can act in a mask even if they're too scared to speak. I also used masks in John Arden's *The Happy Haven* in 1960, in *The Caucasian Chalk Circle* for the RSC in 1962, and in the Comedy Workshop in 1963, which developed into Keith Johnstone's Theatre Machine. I returned to them again in 1979 with an improvised play, *An Optimistic Thrust*, for Joint Stock. None of these was an entirely satisfactory piece of work and all involved a conflict between improvisation and the written text. It's not for nothing that the mask is the symbol of the actor's art. Laurence Olivier used to pooh-pooh my involvement in anything so arty, but he is the great mask actor of our time, working inwards from the externals of make-up and costume. When I was about to rehearse *The Recruiting Officer* at the Old Vic I happened to go into the wig department and discovered Olivier, who was to play Brazen, sitting in front of the mirror trying on an elaborate full-bottomed wig tied with bright blue bows, his false nose already moulded. Whether it was the right image for Farquhar's 'bluff fellow with a sash' I don't know, but I understood that he couldn't start work until he knew what he was to look like. Masks symbolize the actor's independence from the disciplines of the writer and his claim to have a separate art.

Masks have their own rules, stricter than those of everyday acting. A masked actor can never speak as himself, only in the character he has created – or been endowed with – according to how you interpret the process of transformation; he can't read from a script or discuss his motivation. Sometimes he can't speak at all. One of the actors in *An Optimistic Thrust*, Christian Burgess, had created a clumsy, retarded figure, an overgrown schoolboy in shorts and tie. The mask was a full mask, but with a mouthpiece, that Chris had made himself. More than any actor I know Chris can sustain a state of dream existence, but he has never fully understood the expressive life of the voice. Perhaps that's why his character couldn't speak. All I could think of in my search to help him was a scene from the film *Mandy* in which a deaf-mute is taught to speak beginning with the letter B. In one lunch break I threw a ball to Chris's mask, shouting 'Ball.' Very gradually he started to repeat my words; it was a slow process, with many blocks and regressions. Ever after the ball was part of his character and he took it everywhere with him. Was this a piece of arty self-delusion on both our parts? I don't think so. We were attacking the very nature of acting in a sustained improvisation in which we both accepted the rules. Keith Johnstone in his book *Impro* writes convincingly about states of possession in the mask, drawing on anthropological material. I don't go with him all the way. Certainly I have seen some strange and violent revelations in improvisation but I see these more as a release of unconscious urges which are triggered by the concealment of the face rather than the possession by an alien spirit. The mask is the equivalent of the part the actor has to play and in some intuitive process he identifies with something in the nature of the mask. The same mask will produce different characters on different actors, though it will never completely change, and a mask that has seemed a dud will suddenly come to life in response to the right actor. All these processes parallel stages in the conventional building of a character over a rehearsal period, ending with the assumption of costume, wig and make-up in the dress rehearsal.

This way of teaching mask work was, I suspect, more extreme than Saint-Denis or Devine had envisaged. The problem of using masks in a written play were immediately apparent when I directed Arden's *The Happy Haven* in 1960. Arden had written what he hoped was a modern Jacobean comedy set in an old folks' home. The theme of the play was a search for the elixir of life and the old people were played by young actors in masks, with the Doctor, played by Peter Bowles, unmasked. One might have thought that the device would lead to the old people unmasking when they are rejuvenated. Instead they reject the elixir and give it to the doctor instead who reappears, masked, as a baby. The rehearsal process began with improvisations but not in the characters of the play, to develop basic methods of working. Gradually we fed in the masks that the designer had created in further improvisation. Already we had broken the integrity of the process. The designer was trying to create from the writer's text characters that would provide the intuitive stimulus to the actor to create that part. The masks were good but couldn't be guaranteed to provide either exactly what the author had imagined or what would precisely stimulate the individual actor. Even more difficult was the approach to the text. Arden had written a dense, rich, imaginative prose in the style of Ben Jonson. The actors had to learn it sufficiently well for it to be fluent, but without characterizing it. Then they put on their masks and said it in character. A preparation for this was getting the actors to speak something they knew very well, such as a piece of Shakespeare, first, as they would say it unmasked and then in character. Once in character the text becomes distorted, the rhythm disappears, huge pauses are introduced, a single phrase will become highlighted out of all proportion to its significance in the original text. I remember Susan Engel, using a speech of Emilia from *Othello*, in the character of a disgusting old hag called Splodge, pausing when she came to the phrase 'and though we have some grace' and filling it with a terrible consideration of her own ugliness. The text lives as it never would in a production of the play but such intensity breaks both the flow and the thought development of the speech, the scene and finally the play. No writer is going to let the actors so consistently twist and dominate the writing and no director can actually hold up the action of the play. So compromises are made to maintain the balance and in the process the acting loses some of its potency and the masks become another form of stage make-up.

Comic masks, and these are essentially comic masks, resent narrative. They just want to play, to exist, to be, rather than 'to do, to act and to perform' which the Gravedigger in *Hamlet* sees as the three parts of action. Brecht's plays are moral parables in which action, what people do, is demonstrated through a carefully controlled narrative. In *The Chalk Circle* he used masks but more symbolically, in his rather old-fashioned view of good and evil. The bad characters whose lives had been hardened by wrong-doing wear masks, the good, untouched characters like Grusche and Simon Chachava don't. And this I followed in my RSC production in 1962. One of the interesting by-products was that I actually cast some of the play on the basis of improvisations (though as is usual in these circumstances the principals had already been cast) seeing qualities in actors that I would not have seen otherwise. During the course of the rehearsal period my concentration swung away from the intuitive world of masks on to the creation of a dialectic method suitable for a Marxist writer.

I still have not resolved the question of how to use the intense theatricality of masks in a finished piece of work. In 1979 I returned to the problem in *An Optimistic Thrust*, a fully improvised play with a small group of actors for Joint Stock. In a workshop period away from the pressures of time it should have been possible and the work during that period was mind-blowing, but there was a point where it became an examination of the actors' personalities, almost a therapy and bordered on psychodrama and *gestalt*. I drew back from pushing this through and so, I think, did the group. An American group would have gone all the way. Being British we turned towards comedy and literature. The final scene was a cricket match played with quotations from Shakespeare and Dickens. We believe in language, literature, ball games and comedy.

The Brecht play led to a different kind of improvisation, that of the Epic Narrative. I began the rehearsals as I often do, not with ideas about the staging of the work but in finding ways of discovering, with the actors, the author's intentions and how his ideas are translated into terms of theatre. This would be as true for Shakespeare as for Brecht, but the latter is more recently dead; we know what his own productions of his plays were like and he left a great body of theory about his work in untranslatable German. We knew there was something called *Verfremdung Effekt*, quite wrongly translated as 'alienation', and the important thing was to search for the *gestus*, but as with Stanislavsky it was not clear how to apply these in the preparation of a show for the RSC, even though I had insisted on an eight-week rehearsal period (at that time unheard of except by cranky foreigners like Saint-Denis). I decided to begin with a simple Socratic dialogue. I cadged a cigarette from one of the actresses (at that time I smoked like a chimney) and then asked the group why she had given me the cigarette. The first answers were all psychological – her generosity, her syco-phancy, my meanness. Very gradually I led them to under-stand that the action was a social action and a habitual one, in which the economic value of the cigarette was a factor. This led to very simple improvisations which were always followed by an analysis of the actions in the scene. In a two-handed scene each actor would narrate the actions as objectively as possible, sometimes in the third person, and this narration was analysed over and over again till both actors would agree on the exact sequence of events; that is, they would tell the same story. So accustomed were the actors to seeing action from the point of view of their character that this often took a long time.

The next stage was to tell the narrative before the scene so that the end of the improvisation and the actions by which it was reached were already known. This is the antithesis of a Stanislavsky improvisation where only the individual drives or objectives are known and the outcome is still in doubt. In Brecht the focus is on how the decisions are reached and how the actions could be altered. His first, dialectic plays are concerned with alternatives (*Der Jasager* and *Der Neinsager*) and in *The Chalk Circle* the moment of decision is everything. Grusche sits by the abandoned baby through a whole night before falling for 'the temptation of goodness' and taking the baby with her. The Storyteller narrates what she is feeling. Grusche just sits there. When the actor narrates what he will do, rather than what he has done, he starts to feel responsibility for his actions as himself as well as as his character. Interestingly this moment of moral decision also provided the essence of Edward Bond's plays. In *Saved, Narrow Road to the Deep North* and *The Bundle*, a character has to decide whether to pick up the baby or not.

I don't suppose Brecht ever imagined his approach translated into improvisation, but I found it valuable. Actors would construct an improvisation through narrative, in turn identifying themselves, then alternately stating their next action before they did it:

A. 'I am a bus conductor.'
B. 'I am a passenger.'
A. 'I collect the fares.'
B. 'I have no money. I refuse to pay.'

At this point the conductor is faced with a decision. What does he do next? He chooses an action. 'I throw the passenger off the bus.' You then analyse in discussion what else he might have done. What are the alternative actions? The more ordinary the situation the better. I point out that turning the other cheek is an alternative action. The field is widened from Marxism to include Christianity and then Zen. How does one arrive at an unthought, unprepared action? The improvisations become simpler, involving a limited number of actions with a conclusion, rather like a haiku. An actress comes on and bows to us ceremonially and says, 'I am a woman whose baby has died.' Another girl comes on, bows and says, 'I am the midwife.' There is a long pause in which nothing is said. What action can follow? There isn't one, only the experience of the two statements. It's full of emotion, but it has not been arrived at emotionally. The actors have followed a ritual exactly as demanded of them, but we have supplied the feeling. Weigel's wordless cry as Courage when she hears her son shot was like that. However hard she emptied herself of personal emotion we still felt for her. In *Galileo* when Ekkehard Schall came on as Andrea to meet the old master who has betrayed science he looked at Ernst Busch as Galileo and turned away. It was a mechanical move but it produced emotion in us. The situation is so powerful that we are conditioned to feel something. The stripping of action to present only its social and economic meaning is not easy. It was only years later in David Hare's *Fanshen* for Joint Stock that we came anywhere near it. I say 'we' because the act of collaboration between Hare, my co-director Max Stafford-Clark, and all the actors, and our use of discussion, analysis and self-criticism as a group, gave the work a dialectical strength. All the actors played more than one part with the result that the focus never lay on one individual. Brecht, for all his belief in the people, concentrated on extraordinary individuals. However hard he tried to demystify them a heroic glamour surrounds them.

Gradually I got used to seeing a play as a series of actions governed by decisions. A linear concept and one that has altered my perception of drama, not only of Brecht or Edward Bond. During the *Chalk Circle* rehearsals Russell Hunter and Gordon Gostelow, who had played Clarence's murderers in *Richard 111* at Stratford the year before, applied the narrative, descriptive method to the scene. It had never really worked in performance and as we looked at it differently (and this is what *Verfremdung* means) we came to realize that it was because the actors had approached the parts from the erroneous standpoint of individual psychology, in which one was a sadist and the other a coward. As soon as they saw themselves as two workmen earning a living by murder the scene became more real, more interesting and, incidentally, more psychologically accurate. I began to understand that in the theatre it is the action itself that counts, that character is a secondary consideration. Theatre is about what happens, not what people are. But the actor will always pull back towards characterization and the writer move the action forward. The director has to moderate between them.

# 7

# Brecht and
# the Big Ensembles

I left the staff of the Court at the end of 1960 – was I pushed or did I jump? I can't remember. 'The birds are leaving the nest,' George announced. Things were moving in the world outside Sloane Square. Peter Hall was in the process of creating the first full-scale ensemble at the RSC and bringing it to London. He was already eyeing the Court's storehouse of talent and offered Lindsay and me productions at Stratford in the following year – though Lindsay's *Hamlet* never materialized. I was to do *Richard 111* with Christopher Plummer and realized one of my few ambitions by persuading Edith Evans to play Queen Margaret. Jocelyn Herbert agreed to design it. That was another first for me; most of her work at the Court had been with Dexter on the Wesker plays, and with Lindsay on *Serjeant Musgrave's Dance*. This was our chance to bring the Court's version of the Epic style into work on Shakespeare. The RSC was just emerging from a very decorative period in design and Jocelyn worked through endless models of Elizabethan stages and wire cages, which littered the flat in Flood Street, Chelsea, where she lived with George, to create what would be the simplest setting for the play. We eventually arrived at a stage of bare boards – 'It's like a bloody quoit deck, nowhere to sit down,' Dame Edith said – with a single tower, off-centre in the space, and a surround of wire grille. The scenes were marked by very beautiful heraldic emblems lowered from the flies in the Brechtian manner.

After the dress rehearsal there were two figures waiting to give me notes: Peter Hall and George, who could not imagine that our relationship had changed; nor had it. I hurried through my session with Hall to hear what George had to say. Hall's notes were about end-stopping and iambics; George's were practical and on the side of good taste. He particularly hated a fight devised by John Barton, involving Plummer with a ball and chain strapped to his withered arm.

Although I was no longer on the payroll, my relations with the Court were as close as ever. Later in 1961 I ran a company based at the Cambridge Arts Theatre, as a joint venture with the Court. We survived for only three productions, but they included the première of *The Knack*, and introduced Nicol Williamson to the London stage in *That's Us*, one of Henry Chapman's plays set on a building site.

I spent the following year working for the RSC: in Stratford (*Cymbeline* with Vanessa Redgrave), London (*The Caucasian Chalk Circle* with Hugh Griffith) and at a short-lived venture at the Arts Theatre (*Infanticide in the House of Fred Ginger* by Fred Watson, one of the Writers' Group). The improvisations during the rehearsal of the Brecht panicked some of the regular members of the ensemble. Was it getting anywhere, would their performances make the right effect – the usual anxieties of an actor confronted with exploratory methods. A group got together and summoned Peter Hall, who decided to take over in the last stages of rehearsals. Perhaps he pulled the show together, but he completely misread Brecht's specific directions – for instance, the manner in which a poor man eats his only crust. The production was a success, but commercial pressures had been brought to bear. The search for a group approach to a new kind of theatre had been blocked. Again I realized how far I was from the protective, but not uncritical atmosphere of the Court.

After a brief foray into the West End with Brecht's *Baal* starring Peter O'Toole, in the coldest winter ever, I was invited by Laurence Olivier to join him and my old mate, John Dexter, in starting the National Theatre at the Old Vic. Olivier had wanted Devine to join him in the enterprise, but though George was tempted he knew that he would be second in command; at the Court he was in sole charge. I didn't know Olivier, though Joan Plowright had been the Court's first star, promoted by George and Tony over several years. Her relationship with Larry had hit the press while they were rehearsing *Rhinoceros* at the Court, directed by Orson Welles. One reporter even hid in a cupboard in the rehearsal room. When Larry married Joan he also married her interest in new theatre and her loyalties to the actors and directors with whom she had worked.

During the time that I was being sought to work at the National I had started the Royal Court's Actors' Studio at the Jeannetta Cochrane Theatre. Jocelyn had found out that this newly built theatre was not being used until it was opened by Princess Margaret at some time in the future, and we moved in. I had been teaching more and more over the previous two years, and I had started my own improvisation group. Most of this was a development of my work with the writers. The first term was an exploration of comic improvisation: mime with Claude Chagrin, mask work with Keith and myself, and comedians' tricks taught by George. George was a different man when he was teaching. All the cares of running a theatre, which used to show through in his work as an actor and director, disappeared and he returned to his days at the Vic School.

Because this work was so absorbing I was loath to leave it,

even for the glamour and excitement of working with our leading actor in creating a National Theatre. But Larry is not easily put off. His technique, which was absolutely accurate, was to treat me like a woman. I don't think he actually sent me flowers but I was regularly lunched at the Dorchester. 'The wooing of Billy Gaskill,' he called it. Of course I succumbed. Who wouldn't have? But with a proviso that I could continue my studio work at the same time. We even planned for the studio to be open to National Theatre actors but, as in all such plans, the demands of rehearsal always took precedence over class work.

It was not just the lure of working with the man who'd played Henry V that drew me to the National. I was going to be in on the making of an ensemble. The idea of an ensemble haunted all our dreams; it was something that happened only in Europe where they could afford actors under long-term contracts, adequate rehearsal time, and the possibility of developing new methods of acting, direction and design. I'd worked with the RSC, but only as a visitor. Now I was to have the chance to put some of my ideas into practice. The example of the Berliner Ensemble towered over us. Ken Tynan, whom Larry had persuaded to give up criticism and be the first Literary Manager, arranged for us to visit Berlin to see the work of Brecht's company and to meet Helene Weigel. The Oliviers, Dexter, Tynan and myself stood with Weigel at Brecht's graveside in the cemetery that he used to see from his workroom window. In the evening we went to see *Arturo Ui*. We were unanimous in our admiration for the work, perhaps for different reasons. We believed that it set a standard to be emulated, but we never theorized as to how this was to be achieved.

When Larry persuaded Dexter and me to join the National he not only bought our individual talents but the shared viewpoints that came from our training under George Devine. We were suspicious of Tynan, who was obsessed by people of external brilliance and not much else. He also had a great flair for smelling out new movements in the theatre and felt that Dexter and I, as representatives of the Court, were the right associates for Larry. We started to plan the first season. The choice of plays was straightforward: two Shakespeares, an Ibsen, a Chekhov, a Restoration Comedy, a Greek tragedy, a play of the Manchester School and two new plays. Dexter and I both chose plays with a regional background. He was to direct *Hobson's Choice* and I was to do *The Recruiting Officer*.

My choice of the Farquhar was partly influenced by Brecht's version, *Trumpets and Drums*, but it was also the only Restoration play that presented a cross-section of society and which was set outside London. It had no fops, no court intrigue, the leading characters were in the army and even the gentry were not fashionable. At that time the words 'Restoration Comedy' meant high camp, lisps, huge wigs, canes and fans. I didn't consciously set out to alter that; they just seemed unnecessary for the play. No one mentions fans so they were banished; the men looked better in the shorter tie-back hair of a period later than the play so we scrapped historical accuracy. The production was designed by René Allio, Roger Planchon's designer, with whom I had already worked at Stratford. He designed a magical townscape, based on the redbrick Queen Anne buildings of the main street of Amersham. The houses in the setting were three-sided and could transform into a courtroom or the walk by the Severn. It was solid and realistic; witty and flexible.

The choosing of the company was exciting. The Arts Council grant to the National made it possible, for the first time, to pay reasonable salaries to the actors in a classical company; not up to West End standards but higher than they had ever received at the Old Vic or Stratford. I knew it was essential to have Maggie Smith as Silvia. I had first seen her at the Old Vic as Lady Pliant in *The Double Dealer*. It was immediately clear that she was the natural heiress to Edith Evans as the mistress of Restoration Comedy. She was already a West End star but was tempted by the prospect of playing Desdemona and Hilda Wangel, two parts for which she was not obvious casting. Olivier was to play the showy supporting part of Brazen, Bob Stephens and Colin Blakely, both essentially Royal Court actors, were Plume and Kite; Lynn Redgrave, Rose; Michael Gambon, a servant.

I didn't consciously think that this was an oddly assorted group. An exciting actor is an exciting actor and to have several in the same company can only be good. The venture, the newness of the play and the combination of talents meant that the hierarchy that can strangle an ensemble didn't set in. Even so, I knew that the group needed fusing. I started with the simplest of group games sitting in a circle, the traditional party ice-breakers. I approached the text by reading a scene through once, and then improvising it. (At Stratford when I'd asked Edith Evans if she would mind improvising, she looked at me with her asymmetrical eyes and said, 'Is that what William Poel would have called paraphrasing?' And in a sense it was.) It's a method that shows how much an actor has understood of a scene and, more importantly, what has interested him. What is left out is as significant as what is remembered. We also improvised scenes outside the play, particularly for social background. Larry was determined to show he was one of the boys by improvising along with everyone else. I think he hated it but didn't show it. Max Adrian, who was playing Balance, made his unhappiness quite plain.

The production was hailed as a breakthrough in the presentation of period comedy. All I had tried to do was to make the

text sound as if it was being spoken by real people in recognizable situations, to remove anything that came between Farquhar's text and the audience's understanding. The intention
of the play is not political, but there are scenes that present a
political situation as accurately as the most committed writer
could. The scene in which Plume and Kite between them
manipulate Pearmain and Appletree into joining the army is as
good a demonstration of jingoism as I know; the peasants are
not stupid, but they are uneducated and fall for nationalism,
sentimentality and violence as readily as soldiers going to the
Falklands War. Blakely's earthiness and Stephens's cynical
charm were of a new school of acting, which came directly
from their work in Sloane Square.

In the second season I was foolhardy enough to tackle
*Mother Courage*. It is a great play and we were right to do it. But
it was impossible for me or Jocelyn Herbert, who designed it,
to forget the Ensemble's production, nor did we want to.
Brecht's direction of his own play, which was the Ensemble's
first production in 1949, was the product of years of thought
and preparation, a fulfilment of all the work he had left
unfinished in the Germany of the thirties. Every moment,
every image, was honed down to its simplest and most
meaningful statement; its effect was both political and aesthetic. You cannot add anything without destroying that
economy. There are many people who say, 'Throw away the
politics, get rid of the theory, treat Brecht like any other
writer, make him theatrical.' In practice this means filling the
stage with smoke, rock music and punk hair-dos, and the
essence of the work is lost. There may be a time in the future
when we will have to dissociate a Brecht play from its politics,
but perhaps by then the plays will have lost their potency and
will need rewriting, just as he rewrote *The Beggar's Opera*.

But though I had no alternative to following Brecht's

arrangement of the stage the experience of the play comes through the acting. We had no obvious actress to play Courage at the National – you're lucky if there is one in the country at any one time – and I cast Madge Ryan, in a part for which she was not suited. Tynan had fancy ideas about Anna Magnani but I was opposed to his star policy and I knew Madge would be an excellent actress in our ensemble. But I discovered that even in Brecht you need stars. Young Mike Gambon played Eilif, another piece of miscasting, and although there were some fine performances from Frank Finlay as the Cook, Lynn Redgrave as Kattrin and Colin Blakely as the Sergeant we couldn't achieve the character acting in the smaller parts, which is so impressive in the state theatres of Europe. More importantly, for the actors the play was just another play in the repertoire of the company; there was no common attitude, political or aesthetic in the work. I don't think that the Berliner Ensemble was made up of dedicated Marxists, but they were part of a team committed to left-wing plays, written by their director and acted by players like Weigel and Busch who had been refugees from Hitler's Germany. Obviously, we couldn't re-create those circumstances, but without some shared approach to the content of the play the theatrical experience is less. It was only years later, when working for Joint Stock, that I realized that this could be achieved only by a small group of committed actors working closely together on one project.

George was a guest director in the first season for Beckett's *Play* in a double-bill with my production of *Philoctetes*. He came under pressure from Tynan, who understood nothing of responsibility to a writer, to play the piece at a more normal speed than the breakneck pace demanded by Beckett. George would have none of it. I think he felt that we were starting to sell out. Perhaps he was right. In 1964 he had his first heart attack and approached me about taking over the Court, but I was too involved with what I felt was going to be the socialist ensemble of my dreams to be tempted. In the second season at the Vic we had Noël Coward trying to get Dame Edith to remember her lines in *Hay Fever*, Franco Zeffirelli camping it up in *Much Ado*, and a set for *The Crucible* that looked like a gnome's tea party. I could see the socialist ensemble was not going to happen.

I stayed at the National for two years. It was an exciting time. Above all it was an actors' theatre, as you might expect from a company run by Laurence Olivier. By the end of the two years we had a company as strong as any I have known, capable of splitting in two without loss of quality. My last production was a co-direction with John Dexter of *Armstrong's Last Goodnight* by John Arden, with a company that included Albert Finney, Robert Stephens, and young actors like Ian McKellen, Derek Jacobi, Ronald Pickup and Michael York. Simultaneously Olivier, Plowright, Maggie Smith, Blakely and Finlay were playing in Moscow. Was it a true ensemble? Not in the sense of Brecht's company with its more limited repertoire – our actors had to play everything – and not a group of unknown actors of equal status like Joan Littlewood's Theatre Workshop, but it did have an identity. As the repertoire spread to include writers as diverse as Coward and Brecht this started to disappear. Tynan began to suggest outside directors like Zeffirelli, and Jacques Charon from the Comédie Française for particular shows, and the Court influence started to wane.

Neville Blond, the Chairman of the English Stage Company, had instituted a grim annual event: a lunch for all the critics at the Savoy in the first days of January. At the one in 1965 George announced his retirement. His successor had not been chosen. He made a farewell speech.

'When a man begins to feel he is part of the fixtures and fittings it is time he left. I am deeply tired. The weight of this edifice has driven me into the ground up to my neck, like poor Winnie in Beckett's *Happy Days*. I should have passed the job on several years ago. I am getting out just in time.'

When he had finished there was a polite vote of thanks from some nonentity and it looked as if the lunch was over. Lindsay, who had been more critical of George than any of us, but who had a very deep emotional sense of occasion, got to his feet and, after an introductory anxiety cough began, 'I cannot let this occasion go by so unremarked . . .' By the end of his speech he was in full panegyric: 'This wonder, this phenomenon.' There was real applause and some moron started up 'For he's a jolly good fellow'. A few tears were shed and though the occasion was deeply unreal and shallow, it meant something. George was a phenomenon and his vision had changed the British theatre. It was more important for me to carry on his work than to stay at the National. Soon after I talked to George, who, I think, had always wanted me to take over from him. My appointment was quickly ratified by the Council and I had the job. Larry sent a telegram to George, 'The Lord has given and the Lord has taken away.'

The five years between my leaving the Court and my return in 1965 had been great years for me. I had been involved in the early stages of two large ensembles, the RSC, then still financed by private money, and the National, our first state theatre. I had directed the first major productions of Brecht in Britain, neither wholly successfully. With the help of two great designers, Jocelyn Herbert and René Allio, I had tried to bring new methods of staging to Shakespeare and Restoration Comedy. And I had attempted to use improvisation as part of the rehearsal process. All these were to be significant in my first season as George's successor at the Royal Court.

# 8
## First Season in Charge;
### *Saved*

I was still working at the National while I was planning my opening season. For two years I had been used to a permanent company, plays performed in repertoire, and the elegant and serious presentation of the theatre through its programmes, which, at that time, contained no advertisements, no biographies of the actors, and no 'cigarettes by Abdullah'. The world of the West End, weekly rep and number-one tours was swept aside – not, alas, for ever. In their place were serious articles on the background of the play and well-chosen illustrations from period sources. I was determined the same seriousness should inform our plans for the Court. We would have a resident company playing in repertoire and our programmes would treat our writers – Arden, Bond, Jellicoe and Simpson – as the equals of the masters of the past. There would be no transfers, even if a play was successful, and there would be a true ensemble of all the workers in the theatre; at that time the Court still had a full workshop of carpenters, scene painters and wardrobe staff situated in a warehouse near Blackfriars Bridge.

My first action was to re-establish contact with the writers, whom I'd rather lost sight of during my time at the National. On a shelf in the script department was the script of *Saved*, marked 'possible Sunday night'. I had already decided to include a Bond play in the opening season and had provisionally slotted in *The Pope's Wedding*, which had been seen for only one performance. I read *Saved* straight through with absolute absorption. There was no doubt about it. It was a masterpiece. Like the boy in *The Rocking Horse Winner* I was 'sure, O, absolutely sure'. Simpson had also written a play for the new season, *The Cresta Run*, which it was assumed I would direct, but I was resolved to do *Saved* and Keith Johnstone took on the Simpson play. I had a party for all the Court writers in my flat in Clapham Common and they all came apart from Osborne. Edward arrived late with his flies wide open, which was prophetic but not, I think, intentional.

I prepared the season in a tiny room behind George's office which also served as his dressing room during the run of *A Patriot for Me*, in which he played Baron von Epp, the hostess of a drag ball. He was as excited and as idealistic about my season as if it had been his own, nine years before. He never once tried to discourage me from playing in repertoire or having a company. Instead he took me through the whole process of budget-making, of which he was a master. During the run of the play he had another heart attack and was rushed to hospital. He made a temporary recovery but by the time we were in rehearsal he was critically ill. He never saw any of the productions and though he was released from hospital I didn't see him again till just before his death.

The first play in the season was Ann Jellicoe's *Shelley* which she was to direct herself. Once again she and I were choosing a company of actors together. They were three oddly assorted plays. *Shelley* had to be cast with some reference to historical accuracy and we persuaded a very young Ron Pickup to leave the National to play the poet; the Simpson play needed older actors with experience of comedy and Keith somehow managed to get Celia Johnson to play the wife and Sebastian Shaw the man from MI5. Celia didn't stay the course and was replaced by Avril Elgar, but Sebastian stayed for the whole season and fathered the company with exquisite tact, which he must sometimes have found difficult. *Saved*, apart from the mother and father, demanded very young actors, who could also play parts in *Shelley*. Edward was at all the auditions. One of the actors we were very keen to have in the company was Victor Henry, who'd already played in Peter Gill's first D. H. Lawrence production. Victor was burning with talent and self-destruction in almost equal parts. He arrived with one of his spectacles cracked and held together with sticking plaster, his eyes blazing with enthusiasm, and stormed his way through the audition in that wonderful, rasping north-country voice. At the finish he said, 'Like your play, Mr Bond.' 'Humph,' said Edward and crossed him off the list. Perhaps his farouche style would have split the play open. Instead we had John Castle, no less passionate, but heavily concealed. The first Pam was the pale and lovely Barbara Ferris. No one wanted to play the mother, all the actresses we approached were horrified at having a young man mend their stockings while they were wearing them. Gwen Nelson, who had been so great as the mother in *Roots*, had no qualms. 'Shall I audition in my slip?' she said. She got the part. The company included Dennis Waterman, 'mad' Jack Shepherd in his first job, Frances Cuka, Nerys Hughes and Bernard Gallagher.

I decided to have two associates. It had worked well at the Vic and should be imitated. The choice of the associates was, I'm afraid, schematic rather than intuitive or emotional. My closest friends, both directors at the beginning of their careers, were Peter Gill and Desmond O'Donovan, who was also my lover, but I chose neither of them to work with me. Instead I asked Keith, who had directed only Sunday nights at the Court and had no other theatre experience, and Iain Cuthbertson, a great Scots giant, whom I'd met in Glasgow where he was running the Citizens' Theatre (he had been the original Armstrong in Arden's play). Keith was to be the committed, uncompromising voice and Iain was to stand for traditional and popular theatrical values. They are both very large, very emotional men and I don't think I have the coolest of heads. The combination was disastrous. Iain was very nervous of the intellectuals of the Court and delayed directing a play till nearly the end of the first season. Instead he became a leading actor in the ensemble. Keith was never really happy as a director and wanted to develop his theories of comedy and improvisational theatre.

Also directing was Jane Howell, whose good sense and talent did much to fuse the conflicting energies of the company and the staff, and I asked Helen Montagu to be the General Manager. Helen was a raven-haired Australian actress who had joined our Actors' Studio, where she did brilliant improvisations of dismembering children. We became close friends. She had been the Casting Director during George Devine's last year, one of the list of brilliant women who have filled that job. Her energy, warmth and ruthlessness sustained me during all the time I ran the theatre.

After a competition organized by Peter Gill, John Gunter was chosen as the resident designer. The plays were to be performed in repertoire with a twice-weekly change-over in a theatre without wings or storage space. Most of it lived up in the grid, above the stage. I think John was intimidated by three puritanical directors and the whole ethos of the Royal Court. The result was a lot of rather muddy-looking flats. Gunter is a meticulous model-maker, which was just as well as Edward is a demanding author, with a very clear image of what he wants to see on the stage. John made perfect miniature reproductions of the pram and the boat in the second scene. (Edward: 'It's the wrong colour.') The first scene had a central flat with a single door in it which was to serve both drawing room and bedroom. This simple Brechtian device was already a commonplace, but Edward wanted the door to be set back in two angled flats 'like a bowling alley'. Edward has always worked, talked and now directs in similes and metaphors, often tiresomely so. There is, however, as he was quick to point out, only one simile in the whole play, when Harry, the father, describes the man he shot in the war 'like a coat fallin' off a 'anger, I always say'. He also said, 'The only rhetoric in the play is in the last scene,' which was rather perverse since the last scene, apart from one line of Len's, takes place in absolute silence. I took it to mean it was the only structure that had been artificially built up to create a particular effect on the audience. His ear, as well as his eye, is acute. 'When Harry says, "Nigh on midnight," and Len says, "Gone," it must sound like the first stroke of midnight.' I thought to catch him out: 'Like "forlorn, the very sound is like a bell"?' 'In "Ode to a Nightingale" . . . Yes.' I was wasting my time.

By 1965 we had already absorbed the verbal experiments of Beckett and Pinter, Simpson and Jellicoe and the spare, short-line dialogue of *Saved* was immediately accessible. On the surface it was an entirely realistic play. The subject matter, which included the stoning of a baby in its pram, had never been seen on the stage before, nor the scene in which Mary has her stocking mended. But, like all Edward's plays, the choice of the scenes that make up the play is entirely original and not reminiscent of any other writer. The narrative progresses between the scenes. It is only gradually we become aware of what has happened in the interim. Len picks up Pam in scene one; by scene two, the idyllic scene in the boat, he is living in her house; by scene four she is already sleeping with

Fred the boatman, and is estranged from Len. In the middle of this scene, in one of the pauses while Len is eating and the rest are watching telly the baby starts to cry and cries for several minutes before anyone speaks. No one reacts to it. It has not even been mentioned; we don't know whose it is. Gradually in the dialogue that follows we learn that it may be Len's, but Pam denies it. Then Fred appears. As theatre craftsmanship it is masterly, yet it never appears forced or contrived and it puts the dramatic emphasis where it should be – on the actions surrounding the crime, the crime of the lack of love. All the detailed stage directions of Mary's exits and entrances, the setting and clearing of the table, are preparatory to this one extended moment of the baby crying. In its delicacy and clarity it reminds me of Chekhov; in its concentration on precise physical actions relentlessly performed it is like a Noh play; in its awareness of imminent violence offstage it is like a Greek tragedy. When I revived the play in 1969 after the abolition of the censor, and all the publicity over the violence of the baby-stoning scene had died down, it became clear that it was this scene in which the real crime is committed.

*Shelley* opened the season to disastrous notices, which were matched by those for *The Cresta Run* a week later. Everything now hinged on *Saved*. I think I was still naïve enough to think that quality would surely be recognized, but apart from Ronald Bryden in the *New Statesman* it was savaged. The accumulated bile of the critics was vented on the play and on me for presenting it and the whole season. Whereas in 1956 *Look Back* had been patronizingly dismissed, *Saved* was loathed. Nothing is quite like the critics when they are morally outraged. There followed an unparalleled demonstration of solidarity in the profession. Olivier wrote a wonderful letter to the *Observer* comparing the play to *Macbeth*. Ken

Tynan organized a teach-in at the Court at which Mary McCarthy said, very perceptively, that Len had the same basic morality as Cliff in *Look Back*. I demonstrated how Edward's writing distanced itself from violence in the scene where the mother hits the father with the teapot. The play continued to be a talking point and did better business than the other plays. The outrage died down, but then the censor decided to intervene.

At a time when censorship has begun to take a different form under Margaret Thatcher – politicization of the Arts Council, direct interference in the BBC – the tales of the visits to the Lord Chamberlain in his dusty little office in St James's Palace, the bandying of arguments about the validity of 'shit' or 'Christ' and the presentation of alternatives, must now seem rather quaint and harmless. But to us at the time it was a tremendous battle with a real enemy. Like the Dragon in Schwarz's play, which we presented a few years later, censorship has several different heads. The Lord Chamberlain version was the old-fashioned, harmless and stupid English gentleman (though, it must be said, advised by bishops), but he was limiting not just the scope of what could be shown on the stage, but the strength and vitality of the language. Before we submitted the play George Devine read it and suggested a plan of action for the Lord Chamberlain. When the play was returned it was obvious that, whatever concessions Edward was prepared to make on the odd word, he could not and would not rewrite the two scenes that gave offence. Earlier in the year the Court had evaded the censor by presenting Osborne's *A Patriot for Me* for club performances, and I suggested to the Council we should do this for *Saved*. The Council, who had read the play, were completely behind it and me. The only snag was that we were presenting plays in repertoire and we were very keen that the club image should not harm the chances of the other two plays. So many people already thought the Court was a club theatre that we had to take a special ad in the programme in big black letters saying THIS IS NOT A CLUB THEATRE. One night I was stopped in the foyer. 'Mr Gaskill?' 'Yes.' 'We are police officers. Could we have a word with you?' The inevitable had happened. 'Are you responsible for putting on this play?' 'Yes, I did direct it and I am the Artistic Director of the company.' Then I shut up.

When the case came to a hearing at the magistrates' court – it was immediately transferred to a larger courtroom because of the demand for seats, and eventually ran to three separate hearings – the big guns were rolled out in our defence. On trial were: Greville Poke, the Secretary of the English Stage Company, a timid and respectable ferret; Alfred Esdaile, the lessee of the theatre and a former music-hall comedian, to whom lying was second nature; and myself. As witnesses, the Earl of Harewood (a founder member of the company and cousin to the Queen) and Laurence Olivier. After Larry had taken the oath in faultless diction he was asked his occupation. 'I am an ac–tor, sir, and at present Director of the National Theatre' – as if to say 'and tomorrow I shall be lucky to be touring in Scunthorpe'. At the final hearing the magistrate, with theatrical abandon, said, 'I am tied to the rock of the law waiting for some Perseus to rescue me.' By which he meant that the law said we shouldn't have put the play on, even if we were a club theatre, and we were found guilty, but conditionally discharged. Fifty guineas fine. By this time the play had clocked up a tidy number of performances and had done its allotted time in the repertoire. The Council had been rock solid in their support and had refused to withdraw the play in spite of heavy pressure. During the hearings the issue had been debated in the House of Lords and we had peered down from the gallery while the Lords Spiritual and Temporal talked about us, though as Gerald Gardiner, the Lord Chancellor, had pointed out, the case was still *sub judice*. The *Saved* affair had brought to a head the case against the Lord Chamberlain's power of pre-censorship. The following three years were dominated by the fight to break this power, a fight we eventually won.

# 9

# George's Death;
## *Macbeth*

The failure of the first three plays, in particular the violence of the attacks on *Saved*, unified the theatre as nothing else could have done. The season continued to poor houses; Jane Howell directed a revival of *Serjeant Musgrave's Dance* which did better, and my production of Middleton's *A Chaste Maid in Cheapside*, rewritten by Bond, had some good performances, including that of Victor Henry, who had now joined us.

The period was clouded by the thought of George, who was recovering from the stroke he had had during *A Patriot for Me*. Jocelyn let me see him very briefly after he had returned to the flat in Flood Street. The stroke had twisted his mouth so that the voice, always rasping, drilled into me. He made a comment on each of the plays; of *Shelley* – 'You should never have let Ann direct her own play'; of *The Cresta Run* – 'You are our Simpson director'; and of *Saved*, which he'd never really liked – 'I knew they would say it was like that other play' (*Infanticide in the House of Fred Ginger* which I'd directed at the RSC). He made only two other comments; with sudden vehemence, 'What about those buggers? (he meant the Arts Council), and, last of all, very emotionally, 'It's such a beautiful theatre.' That was the last time I saw him. Soon after he had his final stroke.

None of us knew quite how to behave at the funeral. I went

in a taxi with Keith and Sam Beckett. We'd forgotten the address of the crematorium. 'Hoop Lane,' Sam said. We waited in a dreadful little room until the door opened and a formally dressed figure beckoned us. It was Olivier, looking like an undertaker; he always knew how to transform himself. Inside we had to endure some boring piece of the *War Requiem*, which seemed wholly inappropriate for George but it was not quite the thing to play the Modern Jazz Quartet, which we did later at a tribute on the stage of the Court. There was added tension because Sophie, George's wife, and Jocelyn, his mistress, were both there and we felt that where we sat in the chapel was a declaration of our loyalties. The tensions of years were compressed into the occasion. George was only fifty-five and it was difficult not to think that the work had killed him.

The tribute was altogether a more relaxed occasion. I sat on the stage with Edith Evans ('I knew him first, you know'), Peggy Ashcroft ('No, she didn't. I worked with him at the OUDS the year before'), Osborne, who quoted the passage of Dorn from *The Seagull* with which George identified, and Joan Plowright spoke of her days at the Vic School. Lindsay stage managed the occasion as only he knows how. I felt like a very inadequate understudy to a great star and had to introduce the Award that was being started in George's name. Later that year we staged an evening at the Old Vic to raise funds for the Award. Dexter re-created the serving scene from *The Kitchen* with practically all the stars in the British theatre and I revived scenes from *One Way Pendulum* and *The Happy Haven*. The dress rehearsal was memorable, the famous sitting in the stalls waiting to go on the stage. I turned round to find Larry sitting behind me in his Archie Rice make-up, that ridiculous mask with the Robey eyebrows and the gap-tooth. 'This is the real me,' he said.

George's death coincided with the court case over *Saved* and my attempts to salvage the season. Donald Howarth said it would have been inappropriate for me to have had a success at such a moment. There wasn't time to reflect on George's importance to me or the theatre, great though they were. He has since become what Howard Brenton has called 'a secular saint', invoked to remind us of the values we should have and it's hard to dissociate my real memories from that image. He loved the craft and tradition of theatre but he wasn't at all sentimental about the past. I remember him jabbing his finger at Lilian Baylis's roll-top desk (now in the Theatre Museum), which Olivier used to keep in his dressing room at the Old Vic. 'The first thing I would do, Larry, if I were you, would be to get rid of that.' George never liked Baylis, not least because she'd greeted him after his only juvenile performance – as Posthumus Leonatus – with 'Well, dear, you've had your chance and missed it.' But I think he didn't like what she stood for either – a popular theatre without real standards, and Guthrie, who succeeded Baylis, was tarred with the same brush. Guthrie had also been responsible for destroying the Saint-Denis dream of a Theatre Centre at the Old Vic and was never forgiven. George cherished that dream of what theatre might be – actors studying Noh theatre and *commedia dell'arte* to develop their stylistic awareness of texts – but his achievement at the Court was to suppress it in favour of the demands of the new writers.

Perhaps his greatest ability was his belief in other people, not as valuable properties but in their potential. He once said to me about Keith, 'Oh, we may have to wait five years to see anything at all,' and he was prepared to wait that long. Everything in his life was based on personal response to the friends he worked with, to Saint-Denis, Richardson, and then to all of us. We were his children, often disloyal, quarrelling, but we belonged to him. I often dream about him, always the same dream. He has recovered from his stroke and comes back to the theatre, a very benign figure and I don't know how to tell him that I've got his job. We were all lucky to know such a man.

The repertory season carried on with revivals of *The Knack*, Keith's play, *The Performing Giant*, and, for our tenth anniversary, Jane's production of *The Voysey Inheritance* by Granville-Barker. The last play of the season was my production of Wesker's *Their Very Own and Golden City*. The succession of crises had put a considerable strain on the company. There were violent, passionate rows during drinking sessions in the dressing rooms. Arnold's play was written for the principal character to be played by two actors, one young and one mature. Victor Henry was the young A. W. and Ian McKellen had joined us to play the older. It soon became clear that it would be much more sensible to have both parts played by McKellen – Victor was in other plays in the season. At the dress rehearsal Dennis Waterman, who had a small part, was missing. From the fly gallery there was a shower of broken glass. Victor and Dennis were pissed out of their minds and crashing into lamps. Dennis was sacked and replaced by Ken Cranham in his first job.

I liked the play less well than Arnold's earlier work. It is often sententious, and Arnold's dramatization of his own failure at Centre 42 is overstated. My determination to be loyal to the original members of the writers' group had not been productive. What should have been obvious from the experience of George's own first season is that you cannot create a unified ensemble style from the new plays of very different writers, however sympathetic they may be to each other. The ties that had bound us together sitting by Ann Piper's fire in the room by the river were no longer strong.

Then we were all beginners and were excited by this new theatre we were working for. Now Wesker, Simpson and Jellicoe were struggling to maintain their development as individual writers. None of their plays was as bold or imaginative as their earlier work. There was certainly no political ideology holding us together and though we shared some aesthetic principles they were not enough to create an ensemble. The most important work had been Bond's and it was *Saved* that had given the season its character.

After *Golden City* the company disbanded and the theatre reverted to straight runs. Many of the actors continued to work for the theatre on an *ad hoc* basis and provided a strong element of continuity. Most of Victor Henry's career was spent at the Court till the dreadful accident that cut it short and finally brought about his death. Jack Shepherd, Ken Cranham and many others became key figures in the seasons that followed. The first straight run was of Iain Cuthbertson's version of *Ubu Roi* starring Max Wall and designed by David Hockney, his first work for the theatre. Hockney's hair was bleached and with his huge glasses and not dissimilar features he looked like the ghost of George Devine as he peered from the back of the circle at the re-creation of his brush strokes on the backcloth. 'I didn't think they'd copy it exactly.' The production was an odd mixture, but David's work and Max Wall's craftsmanship were unforgettable.

The triumvirate of Cuthbertson, Johnstone and myself had not worked. I decided to ask both Keith and Iain to leave. I was still emotionally tied to both of them but our relationship was no basis for running a theatre. I made the mistake of replacing them with Desmond O'Donovan, with whom I was even more emotionally involved but who had had considerable success at the National. The first season had lost a lot of money. By the end we had been carrying a company of twenty-five actors. Nowadays a cast of eight at the Court is large. The annual accounts showed a sizeable deficit – the only deficit during my seven years' stint – and something had to be done. The new season was to start with Desmond's production of David Cregan's play *Three Men for Colverton* but that wouldn't balance the books. I had heard that Alec Guinness was keen to do some stage work and I arranged to meet him.

Alec was suspicious of me. 'I hear you have "Want Days".' '"Want Days"?' 'Yes, you stand in the gallery and make actors shout obscenities at you.' Now, I have used some improvisational techniques in my time but never that one. I reassured him and we started to discuss possibilities, rather timid ones. *A Trip to Scarborough*, *The Silent Woman*, the never-done classics, and then Shakespeare. I mentioned *Macbeth*. The hooded eyes opened and half shut again but the interest was there. It was a bold idea for both of us. Alec's last Shakespeare had been a fascinating but unsuccessful *Hamlet* in 1951. Although a great film star he has never been a leading classical actor like his seniors, Gielgud and Olivier. And Shakespeare was not standard Royal Court fare. Before he would commit himself he insisted on reading the play with me. The only other actor who had done that was Edith Evans.

Oddly for me I did have a visual concept for the production, which dated back to student days and was probably influenced by Guthrie's *Henry VIII*: that the play should be performed in the brightest possible light with no concessions to atmosphere. All sensation of darkness, whether actual or moral, would come from the language. Every action would be scrutinized ruthlessly. Alec responded to the idea. I think he has always had an oriental concept of acting: 'If you do nothing, when you raise an eyebrow it will be like a pistol shot, like the Noh theatre.' The main question for the director of *Macbeth* is how to embody the supernatural without diminishing Macbeth's responsibility for his actions. Joan Littlewood attacked it by putting the witches in Macbeth's mind like a bad dream. Others have followed the Gordon Craig way and stressed the mumbo-jumbo of the play: Lady Macbeth is a witch herself, etc. These are usually the apostles of darkness, who obfuscate rational thought in the smoke gun of the Royal Shakespeare Company. I don't think this dichotomy would have occurred to the Jacobean audience. The play was performed in the afternoon in bright sunlight at the Globe and in the evening at Blackfriars by candlelight. Shakespeare is constantly questioning the validity of 'spherical predominance' while filling his plays with ghosts. If you plunge the play into darkness it shrinks into a rather indifferent horror film; if you rationalize the supernatural images the theatrical potency disappears. I did not want to demystify the play but to concentrate on the power of the verbal and visual images. It was never Epic Theatre and was more like Bond than Brecht.

The casting of Guinness suited the concept. There is a strange, mystic side to that quiet man. No one could call him obvious casting for the part; he is short (though Garrick was a tiny man he reminded me), stocky and not physically very dynamic. It's hard to imagine him unseaming anyone from the nave to the chops. But then he doesn't have to show his prowess as a fighter till the end of the play. Most of the first third he is spellbound by the witches, his wife or his imagination and doing his best to avoid action. I knew Guinness could do that. In the event he was particularly fine in the last part of the play, swinging round the stage with the spread gait of the character in *Tunes of Glory*.

It was his idea to cast Simone Signoret as Lady M. It seemed a wonderful idea; we had all adored her beauty and sensuality in *Casque d'Or* and her emotional power in *Room at the Top*. She, at least, could not be described as Little Miss

Muffet like so many of our leading actresses. I was flown to Paris and driven out to her country house. She, too, was determined to read the play to me and to work through the text before she would say yes. I had no doubts; here was a remarkable actress. The fact that quite apart from her accent she had no experience of the classical theatre might have deterred me. Sitting opposite Golden Marie and eating French cooking was too tempting.

Guinness had decided to play the part with a slight Scots accent so it was natural to cast both Banquo (Gordon Jackson, also new to Shakespeare) and Macduff (a young Maurice Roëves) as Scots. Susan Engel played Lady Macduff and understudied Signoret. As if I had not stuck my neck out far enough already I cast three black actors as the Witches: Zakes Mokae, from South Africa, and Femi Euba and Jumoke Debayo, both Yorubas from Nigeria. They had all been in Soyinka's *The Trials of Brother Jero* directed by Athol Fugard, which I'd enormously admired. It was difficult to justify this casting without sounding racist. Certainly they handled the supernatural without self-consciousness and in their white wigs they looked like something from the Kabuki.

Christopher Morley designed the set. Our aim was to try and create the sensation of a Jacobean hall in which there was a screen with a single door but somehow in the same space as the audience; almost impossible on a proscenium stage. His solution was to place the screen and two side panels inside a surround of the identical material. The surround stretched out of sight; the screen and panels were the same height as the proscenium arch. The Court has unusual proportions: it has a narrow opening, just over twenty-one feet, but it is almost as high as it is wide and, if you include the forestage, deeper. It creates a classic cube, an odd but effective theatre space. The model of the set was made of deep golden sandpaper, floor and walls, and this was re-created on the stage by covering the flat surfaces with wood shavings, glued and painted. Under the heat of the lights the glue made the flats contract and buckle and they were held vertical by ropes fastened offstage. As the run progressed these became more and more taut. The overall effect was of a golden box within a larger box. And the lights beat down relentlessly.

The costumes were originally to be designed by Leslie Hurry, the first stage designer ever to excite me, but, though he did some beautiful sketches and loved Chris Morley's set, his clothes were out of key. A protégé of Chris's, Richard Montgomery, took them over; very muted grey shapes like early tracksuits. Simone was already very thick in bust and hip but still had a waist so we emphasized that. The costumes would look pretty quaint now, but the set was way ahead of its time. The box eventually became the standard format at the RSC. When I showed the model to Alec he was very excited but said, 'Where do I go to murder Duncan?' I pointed to the upstage doorway. 'Oh, no,' he said. 'I would have to play the dagger speech upstage. Can't be done.' We agreed that he should use the down-left proscenium entrance. His re-entrance from the murder was startling. Suddenly he was there, on top of the front row. Like many a Macbeth before him we had worked out (a) that there are two daggers, (b) that Lady M. doesn't see them straightaway, (c) that 'This is a sorry sight' must refer to the blood on his hand; therefore the daggers must be carried in one hand held back from his wife's view. Alec took this further by holding his bloody hand back as well, so that he entered chest first as you might say. When he came to 'This is a sorry sight' he produced the blood-stained hand furtively, close to his body, like a child showing something indecent. Everything about his perform-ance was daring and individual. Though his effects were finally studied he would arrive at them intuitively. 'Perhaps I might dance here,' he said and, as he got to 'now celebrates pale Hecate's offering', he rose on the balls of his feet and sketched in the arm movements of the Highland fling. Our working relationship was very good, though he despaired of some of the other members of the company. One day we were sharing a stall in the men's lavatory and he said, 'I've worked with Guthrie and Komisarjevsky and Saint-Denis and I think you're as good as any of them.' It's difficult to respond to such a compliment when one's peeing.

Simone was wonderful to work with in a quite different way. She was deeply emotional with very little stage technique but at her best she was more immediately real than Alec. She would seize him in her capacious hands when she said, 'Oo woz eet zat zus cried?' and shake him. Alec begged her not to do it so brutally. After one performance he went to her dressing room and pulled up his sleeve revealing an ugly purple bruise. 'Oh, Alec, I'm so sorry.' Guinness took a cloth and wiped off the mark. He had concocted it with greasepaint. Their relationship was strong but they were not in the end the best of partners. The production opened to the most horrendous notices ever, or so it seemed. On the second night Simone's nerve went and she dried. Alec took her and held her till she nodded, said, 'OK,' and went on with the show.

I was foolishly upset by the notices. The critics had been disastrously wrong over *Saved*, which I knew to be a masterpiece, so they must be wrong over my work too. When you direct a new play it's usually the writer who takes the flak but with a classic it's the director or the actors who are on the line. Simone was doomed from the start because of her accent. It's easy to mock, as I have done above, and it brings out the worst side of the English character. Simone, in her autobiography, tells how she wakes with the relief of not playing Lady Macbeth that day. I wrote a violent and rather pompous letter threatening to ban all the critics from future productions. Of course, the freedom of the press was invoked and the critics, who hate being attacked themselves, rose in righteous fury and tried to lose me my job. I had gone to Tunisia on holiday and the phone rang while I was sitting under an orange tree having breakfast. It was the *Daily Express*. I came back at the BBC's expense to defend myself on television and sort things out with the Council, who were very supportive, although they had to make me back down over my threat. Lord Harewood drafted a press statement, as only he knows how, to save my face. It was the second of my crises and I'd only been in the job a year.

# The Importance
# of Phrasing

Acting at the Royal Court was considered just as much a breakthrough as writing. The new plays demanded new playing. To begin with there was a myth that there was a breed of working-class actors in Sloane Square. It wasn't true. But there was a group of actors whose regional background was very clear in the way they spoke and who were not ashamed of it. Most of them came from the North in the early days; the Bond plays seemed to bring out a crop of South Londoners. The directors round the Court had a firm idea of what a good actor was. He was like Wilfred Lawson, the West Riding actor with the gentle, slurred voice who was the idol of Finney (from Salford) and O'Toole (from Leeds). He was considered more real, to have more feeling, than the heartless Olivier. So suspicious were we of what was thought to be external acting that it was even suggested that Olivier should be replaced in the film of *The Entertainer* by Trevor Howard. This belief in a more internal acting was boosted when we heard about the Actors' Studio and how the Method had influenced Marlon Brando. And Angelika Hurwicz as Grusche in *The Chalk Circle* was fat and plain but the centre of the play.

Unquestionably there was a new breed of non-heroic or non-romantic actors. George Devine discovered Colin Blakely in Ireland. My first sight of him was as the

Pugnacious Collier in *Serjeant Musgrave's Dance* pounding away at the stage in a mad clog dance. His recent death has deprived us of one of our best actors. Frank Finlay came to London from Coventry in *Chicken Soup with Barley*. He was unforgettable when he was about to lose control of his bowels. When Joan Plowright leapt on to a chair in *Roots*, it was the image of the working class breaking in to a new life. Cynics might say it represented a class shift, but something had changed. Working-class characters were no longer comic minor roles but the new heroes and heroines.

When these actors moved into the large classical companies they were faced with extending their range and their skills. It was all right having a Scunthorpe accent in *Roots* but not, perhaps, in Shakespeare. I took Colin Blakely to Stratford to play Hastings in *Richard III*. In the scene with Queen Margaret he had to say to Edith Evans:

> False, boding, woman, end thy frantic curse
> Lest to thy harm thou move our patience.

which came out something like:

> Forrlsburrding wumman, ond they frontic corse
> Lesstyew they horm tharr muvarr pazhunz.

Edith would interrupt: 'Oh, no, Colin, you must love all the words. "Faaalse, BOAADING woman . . .".

The process enriched the theatre but did not, I think, alter basic approaches to acting. Neither Finlay nor Blakely became leading classical actors. Finlay's Iago was swamped by the brilliance of Olivier's Othello and Blakely's only major part in Shakespeare was a Titus for the RSC. Shortly before he died he was playing in an Alan Ayckbourn in the West End. He was still a wonderful actor, but no longer the leader of change that we had imagined him to be.

Lindsay Anderson once said of me that I directed classics like new plays and new plays like classics. I can't imagine anything more flattering. It was only through working with living writers that I understood how to approach a classical text, and only by working with classically trained actors that I understood the importance of speaking and phrasing in any play, new or old.

*Macbeth* was an attempt to create a stage in which the text would have a potency usually denied it. I think Beckett's work is a search for what is essential in theatre, as if he would say, 'Theatre is just a person alone on the stage speaking. He doesn't have to move and the language he speaks can be devoid of imagery, colour or social reference, but the situation he is in and his experience of that situation is enough to make drama.' In the progression of his plays the characters become more and more static; Vladimir and Estragon cannot leave the place they are in, Hamm is bound to a chair, Winnie is buried up to her waist and then up to her neck, the three souls in *Play* are in urns; finally in *Not I* there is just a mouth on the stage talking. It's as if Beckett is testing the very nature of drama. The characters must speak even if they are driven to do it automatically and without thought. It doesn't prove they are alive, in fact it's quite likely they are dead and don't know it, but they must speak to make drama.

What is the most famous moment in drama? Hamlet walking on to the stage and saying 'To be or not to be' – a speech that seems to have no relation to the narrative of the play and whose meaning is enigmatic. Just a man in black standing alone on the stage talking. My production of *Macbeth* was an attempt to explore this understanding of theatre, to see if the text would have its maximum potency in a naked space. The bright light and the hot setting would allow the images of darkness to exist more powerfully, as if the play were being performed on a sunny afternoon at the Globe. I hadn't reckoned with the changing nature of an audience's conditioning. They see first, listen afterwards, particularly with an old text where half the words may have lost meaning for them. When Macbeth says, 'Light thickens, and the crow makes wing to the rooky wood,' my scalp tingles. I don't think this is true for many in the audience today. I don't need the electrician to dim the lights to help me; indeed, I feel my imagination insulted if this happens. If the external world doesn't change I can decide for myself whether the darkness is actual or whether the darkness is coming from Macbeth. This must have been true for the Jacobean audience, but is true no longer.

In this changed situation we still have to believe in the potency of language and the expressive power of the actor's voice. Writing has stopped being a succession of images but has acquired a different kind of communication; words may have lost their evocative, picture-making power under the visual onslaught of films and television but they can still delineate situations and people's awareness of them, even in the emotionally concealed world of Pinter. And if phrased and timed properly they still have the power to make people laugh. A university education gave me the ability to analyse a text in terms of structure and meaning but it was working with actors that taught me about phrasing and timing. Great actors like Edith Evans, Alec Guinness and Maggie Smith taught me more about approaching a text than any academic. I detest the tendency of the RSC to become a kind of seminar for Cambridge undergraduates: 'Give me an example of a feminine ending.' '"To be or not to be that is the question".' 'Well done, Ian, go to the top of the class' – what has that to do with theatre? And there are those who talk of 'verse speaking' as if it were some strange and mystic skill, ignoring the fact that a great deal of Shakespeare is written in prose.

Actors are the continuing life of the theatre; they have to go on working even if writers dry up. The classics are always there as a challenge and a lifeline. Actors adapt, work when and where they can, develop new skills with the changing demands of writers and directors. The Court has demonstrated this at all times. A new generation of young actors arrived to fulfil the needs of Osborne, Wesker and the rest but it was Olivier who was the first leading actor of an earlier generation to work there. The ability of a classically trained actor to respond to a text can illuminate new work even if he does not altogether understand it or sympathize with its viewpoint. George was the crucial link between the two generations of actors and his passionate devotion to good writing gave a status to the new dramatists that put them alongside the classics.

When I was a boy I used to have two albums of scratched 78s entitled *The Voice of Poetry*, read by John Gielgud and Edith Evans, the undisputed master and mistress of classical speaking. Their phrasing and cadences are still with me, though the poetry was mainly Romantic and Georgian. Gielgud's control of pitch and inflexion in Ben Jonson's 'The Triumph' is the most beautiful I have ever heard. During my time at Oxford he came to lecture in the Sheldonian Theatre, which is not a theatre at all but the building used for formal university occasions. In his lecture he talked about Evans and her control of the text. One example he gave was from *The Importance of Being Earnest* when Lady Bracknell says this – and he imitated, not Edith's voice but her phrasing –

You can hardly imagine . . . that I and Lord Bracknell . . . would dream of allowing our only daughter . . . a girl brought up with the utmost care . . . to marry into a

1. George Devine and the author at a dress rehearsal of *The Sport of My Mad Mother*, February 1958. (*Sandra R. Lousada*)

2. John Arden's *The Happy Haven*, Royal Court, 1960. Susan Engel as Mrs Phineus, Barrie Ingham as Mr Golightly. (*Roger Mayne*)

3. A mask improvisation during rehearsals of *The Caucasian Chalk Circle*, RSC, 1962. Probably Patsy Byrne. (*Roger Mayne*)

4. *Richard III*, RSC, Stratford, 1961. Edith Evans as Queen
Margaret. (*Angus McBean*)

5. *The Recruiting Officer*, National Theatre at the Old Vic, 1963.
Robert Stephens as Plume and Laurence Olivier as Brazen.
(*Lewis Morley*)

6. Edward Bond's *Saved*, Royal Court, 1965: i The ghost – John Castle and Richard Butler. ii The stoning – John Bull, Bill Stewart, Dennis Waterman, Ronald Pickup, Tony Selby. (*Zoë Dominic*)

7. *Macbeth*, Royal Court, 1966. Rehearsal – the author and Alec Guinness. (*Lord Snowdon*)

8. *Three Sisters*, Royal Court, 1967. Rehearsal – the author, Avril Elgar, Marianne Faithfull, Glenda Jackson. (*John Haynes*)

9. Bond's *Lear*, Royal Court, 1971. The wall – Harry Andrews as Lear. (*John Haynes*)

10. Bond's *The Sea*, Royal Court, 1973: i The author in rehearsal
ii Simon Rouse, Mark McManus, Gillian Martell, Margaret
Lawley, Coral Browne. (*John Haynes*)

11. David Hare's *Fanshen*, Joint Stock, 1975. Phillip McGough addresses the delegates. (*John Haynes*)

12. Heathcote Williams' *The Speakers*, Joint Stock, 1974. Tony Rohr as McGuinness. (*John Haynes*)

waiting room . . . and form an alliance with a parcel. Good day, Mr Worthing.

At the end of each phrase there was no real pause but the clearest of upward inflexions carrying you through the line until the end with a very firm downward one on 'parcel' before the 'Good day, Mr Worthing' and the exit – and the applause; the actress controlled her performance and the audience's reaction by her command of the writing. Wilde's sentences, like Congreve's and Shaw's, are often long but they are the unit of the writer's expression and in consequence that of the actor. I am often asked about period style as if the flick of a handkerchief or the twirl of a cane were the answer. I always reply, 'Start with the text.' Some time between Shaw and Coward people stopped using long sentences, writing became clipped and unemotional, and eventually arrived at Pinter and Bond. But the unit of the sentence, however short, is still the clearest indication of style.

When I came to work with Edith on Queen Margaret she showed me how the grasp of a sentence is as important in blank verse as it is in prose, perhaps more important. Sometimes a long speech in Shakespeare will be made up of just one sentence and the actor must carry the shape, thought and feeling through the speech, pulling himself towards the end. Edith didn't formulate this, though she did give me one tip: 'Ignore the commas, they're not important.' Her understanding of phrasing was based on her ear ('I have perfect pitch, you know') and its relation to her emotional response to the part. The phrases, the sentences, were channels through which the feeling ran. It was important to know technically what the channels were and how to keep them unblocked so that the feeling could have free passage. Often the sentence was expressive of an objective in the Stanislavsky sense, but I would not have interfered with Edith's work process to say this. Analysis would only have been a hindrance. Her relation with the text was very close. She lived through it, under it and above it. Like an opera singer she would launch herself at a line with total concentration. If there was a pause in the rehearsal she would have an intuitive sense of where to pick up the text. 'Could we go back to . . .' I would start, and the voice would be launched at full pitch: 'Thou elvish marked, abortive rooting hog . . .' Once I ventured to suggest an alternative inflexion. 'Oooh, teacher, teacher,' she said on a descending cadence, 'you're quite wrong.'

She never worked at the Court and her only real contact with the new writers was as Ma Tanner in the film of *Look Back in Anger* and as the Squire's sister in *Tom Jones*. It was not that she couldn't play working class; her performances in *The Last Days of Dolwyn* and *The Listeners* prove the opposite, but perhaps the overpowering emotional nature of her acting was too large for the disciplines of Pinter, though she used to say, 'I think I could do it. I am a Cockney, you know.'

Much of my understanding of acting has come from the old stars. Perhaps they developed their craft more gradually over a period of years and came to an awareness that they were able to pass on. Guinness in the rehearsals of *Macbeth* said to a young actor, 'Don't stress your personal pronouns. It's quite wrong.' I learned later that this was a tip he'd picked up from Martita Hunt when she was trying to teach him to act. So many times I've heard an actor stress 'I' rather than the verb that follows and I start a rather boring homily on the subject, which goes something like this: 'If you want to tell someone you love them you don't say *I* love you or I love *you* but I *love* you.' If it's Shakespeare I tell them the natural iambic stress is on the verb anyway. It won't make for great acting but it will clarify the sense, the intention of the line.

Much of the art of speaking is removing the unnecessary, the unnatural stress, allowing the line to speak for itself and the character's relation to the line. Inflexion – or line reading as the Americans call it – is notoriously difficult to teach, even though I am often tempted to do so when an actor shows he has completely misunderstood a line. This is because any line in a play is said by a character in a situation and is not a statement of objective, scientific fact. But – and it's a very big but – a line has a kind of objective life within that context; it may have more than one meaning but it cannot have an infinite number of meanings. I believe an actor intuits the meaning of a line and why the character is saying it in the same moment. For actors like Gielgud and Evans this is very akin to a sense of musical pitch. Tynan once described Gielgud's speaking in the terms that Pope had described a spider spinning a web:

> The spider's touch how exquisitely fine!
> Feels at each thread, and lives along the line.

His perception of the meaning of the line is his alone, but governed by the constant practice of the best classic texts and his respect for them. It's always obvious to me if an actor I am working with has spent much time in television; he interpolates 'wells' and 'buts' all over the place to make, as he thinks, the text more sayable. He is used to clumsily written texts which he has been given *carte blanche* to alter. When he is confronted by the flint-like full stops of Edward Bond or the pauses of Pinter or Beckett he has to be disciplined to respect a text again, in the way he would respect Shakespeare or Shaw or Wilde. In directing I have almost stopped looking at the script and rely on my ear to determine whether a line is right. Punctuation can become a fetish too and it's more important to hear than to follow rules; to hear the writer's rhythms and phrasing and to get the actor to hear and feel his own response to them. The architecture of a speech is built on its punctuation, but its life is governed by the actor's impulses.

# 11

# Three Sisters; Early Morning

Desmond O'Donovan, my new associate at the start of my second season, was another of the large men whom I mistakenly relied on. I would have been better off with tough little terriers like Peter Gill or Bob Kidd. Desmond had been destined for the priesthood by his Irish parents, but after six years in a monastery had collapsed with a nervous breakdown before taking his final vows. When he recovered he transferred his vocation to the theatre and underwent an almost identical cycle. His timeless, dreamy, obsessive manner did not make him an ideal director, but he could sometimes project this quality into his work, notably Peter Gill's first play, *The Sleeper's Den*, and in his work on the Indians in *The Royal Hunt of the Sun*. He contracted hepatitis while he was rehearsing Wole Soyinka's play *The Lion and the Jewel* and I had to take over. Later his cycle of manic depression seemed to be aggravated by LSD. The direction of plays became divided between Peter Gill, Jane Howell and myself. Peter started work on *The Daughter-in-Law*, the second of the plays in what was to become the D. H. Lawrence Trilogy. Jane launched what we called the Schools Scheme with a revival of *Roots*.

We were still waiting for a new play from Edward Bond but meanwhile I asked him to make a version of *Three Sisters*, which I knew he had studied closely, and with Richard

Cottrell's help he made a fine translation. The play had not been seen in London in a British production since 1951 (though we had seen both the Moscow Arts and the Actors' Studio). Olivier was planning a production at the National and plied me with whisky so that I would give up mine. I refused.

It's never difficult to get a good cast together for Chekhov; all the parts are so well written. Glenda Jackson was to play Masha and Avril Elgar, whom I'd worked with many times since her unforgettable Norah in *George Dillon*, Olga. Finding an Irina was much more tricky. *Ingénues* don't grow on trees. I auditioned extensively but could find no one. Someone suggested I should see Marianne Faithful, the girl-friend of Mick Jagger. This deathly pale girl, exquisitely beautiful, arrived. I suppose I'd expected a bit of gorblimey but Marianne is related to the Sacher-Masochs (which now seems only too apposite) and was more than suited to be one of the Prozorovs. She read tentatively but, as Dr Dorn says of Constantin in *The Seagull*, she had 'something'. One of the lines Bond gave to Tusenbach describes her perfectly: 'Your paleness is like a lamp. It makes the darkness shine.' There was a panic on the first day of rehearsal waiting for her Equity membership to be validated and I was later denounced at a union meeting as 'an irresponsible and vicious poseur', but most of the actors accepted her for her talent. She didn't find the discipline of rehearsals easy. A pop star's life is spent in periods of intense activity, mostly through the night, fol-lowed by periods of relaxation and a life-style which, at that time, as now, is often centred in drugs. Marianne had the real actress's ability to transform herself into what was required by whoever she was with. To me she appeared starry-eyed, idealistic and delicate; to Bob Kidd, one of my assistants, she was a trendy slut. I was reminded of the heroine of Henry

James's *The Tragic Muse*. It's a pity her commitment to acting was not great enough to survive the demands of her life-style. The tough, the dull, but above all the committed, survive.

Edward, as usual, had metaphors to describe the play: 'The first two acts are the preparation for the crime; the third act is the crime itself, and the fourth act is the police report'; 'When Olga enters in the third act she should come on as if her skirts were on fire'; 'When Masha says that Natasha goes round as if she had started the fire you should believe her.' I don't know how much of his insight fed into the production but it was fascinating to see the work of a writer of the past through the eyes of a writer of today. The version was spare and sayable. Abd'elkader Farrah's set used the great height of the Court stage and was finally defeated only by the lack of space in the last act. The rehearsal period was very happy, as I imagine it always is with Chekhov. I particularly loved Alan Webb as Chebutkin, who fulfilled Chekhov's stage direction in the last act better than anyone I've known: 'He maintains an air of cheerfulness throughout the act.' The production was my first collaboration with Andy Phillips, the lighting designer who was to light all my shows for the next five years. He absorbed the basic Brechtian approach to lighting and softened it into something of his own. He works on the principle that it is the lighting designer's job to light the actors, and to light them equally. To achieve this he uses a great many lamps, each covering a small area with almost equal intensity, very carefully balanced out. He avoids chiaroscuro but the effect is not unatmospheric. The cool last act of *Three Sisters* was his first statement of the style which was to become the hallmark of Court productions.

The time that followed showed the work of the Court shifting under various influences. The field of writers had thinned out, leaving Bond as the front runner. David Cregan and Donald Howarth were still in the race and David Storey had just entered but the main excitement was coming from the United States. I was persuaded to bring over Joe Chaikin's Open Theater in *America Hurrah*, a trilogy of plays by Jean Claude van Itallie. Suddenly the whole emphasis was back on style, presentation and the work of a group of committed actors. The last play, *Motel*, had actors in giant heads scrawling obscenities on the walls of the set to violent music. In every way it was outside, you could say against, the Court tradition, which had never been defined but was understood by all of us. Later Lindsay Anderson defined it as humanist and, if we'd thought about it, I suppose we would have accepted that. But the naked impact of the Open Theater couldn't be ignored. The work was also extremely professional and stylish. The plays were very successful and were scheduled to transfer to the West End. Because they had not received a licence from the Lord Chamberlain the Court had been turned into a 'club theatre' again, in spite of the *Saved* prosecution. The Chamberlain had turned a blind eye to our breach of the law but there were warning signals that if the play transferred it would be prosecuted. I was about to open the next show, Charles Wood's *Fill the Stage with Happy Hours* at the Court and decided to move it to the West End instead and leave Chaikin's company at the Court. We planned to do another Charles Wood play, *Dingo*, which had also been refused a licence. *Dingo* had strange images of violence mixed with satire and political fantasy. Was the character Henry Woolf played Montgomery or Hitler? Why was Mark Jones kicking a cabbage as if it were someone's head? I couldn't answer these questions. Once again the Stanislavsky method and the dialectic analysis of Brecht seemed of little use. Yet the play was Brechtian in the way it disturbed through its images.

The summer of 1967 was the summer of *Sergeant Pepper*, Mick Jagger's arrest and flower power. It was also the summer in which Joe Orton was bashed to death by his lover. A double-bill of his plays had just been directed at the Court by Peter Gill. Orton was not really a Court writer though after the first, unsuccessful production of *Loot* the play had been offered to the Court just before Devine retired. He didn't care for it and it was passed on to me. I thought it slick but amoral, which it is, but failed to realize how immediate its appeal would be. The Court tradition did not draw back from violence but it was basically moral. Joe felt, probably rightly, that his was a much better play than some of the Court's offerings, however moral they might be. The last time I had supper with him, which he records in his diary as a disaster, he left early to go cottaging. A few days later he was dead.

The whole summer was an upsetting time. The work coming from America was disturbing, demanding social change but not through political action in the left-wing tradition of Arnold Wesker. Pot began to be smoked in the lighting box. It was clear that the Living Theater, La Mama, the Open Theater and the Bread and Puppet Theater, all of whom visited London, some of them at my invitation, were pushing towards anarchy, to a breakdown of structure and towards a form of theatre that was non-verbal or at least non-literary. Literature was a dirty word; realism was dead; theatre must take to the streets. How would our writers respond to these threats or were they already part of the same movement?

By this time I suppose I should have guessed that Bond was not exactly a prophet of social realism. Nevertheless when the script of *Early Morning* arrived on my desk in 1967 I was completely unprepared for the fantasy unleashed: Queen

Victoria and Florence Nightingale as lesbian lovers, two princes, Arthur and George, Siamese twins; a last act in a heaven where everyone eats each other and this is considered morally right. No, I wasn't ready for that. Edward is like a surrealist painter; what he creates *is* real and there is no basic difference for him between *Saved* and *Early Morning*. Originally God was to appear as a huge grey rat. Perhaps the play had been boiling up inside him for a long time; it certainly has the feeling of 'This is what I've ever thought about anything' that you get in *Hamlet* or *Peer Gynt*. Like *Peer Gynt* it is in three parts and each part feels like a separate play. Like *Hamlet* it takes a family relationship and inflates it into a larger statement by pretending the characters are kings and queens. *Saved* was about a loveless family in which the father and mother want to kill each other. In *Early Morning* they have become Prince Albert and Queen Victoria, and the mother succeeds in killing the father. Albert returns like the ghost of Hamlet's father and cries 'Revenge' like an oyster-wife. Arthur, the introvert, inactive half of the personality carries the dead extrovert half round as a skeleton. I hesitate to plough more of the Freudian ground. Florence starts as an *ingénue*, becomes a sadist and ends up near-sympathetic. The symbols come thick and fast; people are brought to life by magic and die again. I might think I was overstating the case if Edward had not admitted he was well aware of the implications of the line when the two princes escape through a small trapdoor, 'We'll escape through Mother's secret passage.' His perverse and witty awareness of his own intentions is both exasperating and charming.

In their clear grey light the images of *Early Morning* were as sharply defined as those of Magritte, or at least they were in Edward's head and on the page. Their realization on the stage was another matter. It was like a film script, with one scene on top of Beachy Head as it collapses, the next on the ground below. In the last act Arthur has to be steadily eaten so that in one scene Florence has only his head left in her lap. Fortunately the Court still has its carefully preserved traps; Florence sat just behind one of the traps with her crinoline covering it, Arthur was brought up just far enough for his head to come through a slit in the crinoline. The end of the play was even trickier: Arthur's body keeps growing again even though he has been eaten; his mother orders his body placed in a coffin and nails down the lid. '*Arthur steps out of the coffin. He stands on the lid . . . he starts to rise in the air . . . his feet are seen.*' How the fuck was I to do this? Even if we could cheat the coming out of the coffin how could we make Arthur fly? We couldn't attach the wire till he was out of the coffin and it would be impossible to mask. Eventually we compromised. We split the coffin lid in half and pin-hinged the halves together. When Arthur was laid in the coffin he was taken down on the grave-trap. The actor removed the pin-hinges and he was brought up on a plinth placed on the trap and in a long white robe which masked his feet. The trap was raised very slowly, the lid fell away and Arthur appeared to be levitating as the curtain fell. That's just one example of how a succession of images formed in the writer's mind has to be made concrete in performance.

Deirdre Clancy, who designed the play, made paintings of the scenes before rehearsals started. This was an idea taken from Brecht's designer, Casper Neher, and the images drawn from the text were wonderfully realized by Deirdre. The bloodless figure of Arthur looks uncannily like Peter Eyre, who played it originally, though he had not yet been cast. Marianne returned to play Florence Nightingale, Jack Shepherd was Gladstone, seen by Bond as a sadistic trade union leader, and Nigel Hawthorne was Prince Albert.

*Early Morning* was too difficult a play to command the same solidarity from the ESC Council as *Saved*. I had been in the job for two years and several crises; the honeymoon was over. The play had been submitted to the Lord Chamberlain who had returned it with a total ban. This was unheard of. Entire scenes had been cut before but never a complete play. It was rumoured that the Queen, who was known to be devoted to the memory of her great-great grandmother, had heard of the imputation of lesbianism and had said, 'Enough is enough.' No doubt bishops were involved too. We knew now that the pretence of a club theatre would be no defence in law if the Lord Chamberlain chose to prosecute, though he had let us get away with *America Hurrah* and *Dingo*. He did not want to be in open confrontation on every minor infringement, as long as the plays were not seen by too many people. But he could not allow open insults to the Royal Family, whose protocol he administered. But the movement against him was gathering force. A Private Member's Bill to end the censorship of plays had been lucky in the ballot in the Commons. It looked as if the dream of Shaw and Granville-Barker was about to be realized. Meanwhile an unlicensed *Early Morning* was scheduled for production. A prosecution in the middle of parliamentary legislation might affect the Bill's chances of success.

I was determined to get the play on at all costs. The forces of the establishment started to move against me. Neville Blond, our Chairman, talked to Lord Goodman, then the Chairman of the Arts Council. The Arts Council said we could not use its grant for an unlicensed play in the main house. It would endanger George Strauss's Bill. I was still battling with the problem when I went down with pneumonia. When I recovered I managed to persuade the Council to let me schedule the play for a series of Sunday night performances, supposedly 'without décor' but actually with as much of Deirdre's design concept as I could sneak by.

Much of this political manoeuvring was going on while I was trying to rehearse an immensely difficult play. It eventually appeared on 2 April 1968, twelve years after the first night of *The Mulberry Bush*. Again the Vice Squad visited the theatre and this time the pressure was too great. The following Sunday's performance was cancelled and an afternoon 'dress rehearsal' for the critics arranged. The public were let in by a side door. One photographer from the *Mirror* managed to get a snap of Marianne Faithful in her kilt as John Brown before he was thrown out. The play was not well received; neither Tynan nor Harewood two of my staunchest allies, was behind it. While this was going on George Strauss had been piloting his Bill through the Commons and it eventually received the Royal Assent in September. The general feeling was that I had been rocking the boat. Deep down I knew you always have to resist the forces of the Establishment even when they appear to be liberal and on your side. For me it was important that the play was done when we wanted to do it and not at a time convenient to Parliament or the Arts Council.

The production had cost £500, considerably more than an average Sunday night. Neville Blond, the Chairman of the Council, started the next meeting with a list of my crimes, this over-spending being the worst, and demanded my resignation. Neville was a remarkable business man who had steered the Court through crisis after crisis. He was completely philistine, with no experience or understanding of theatre, but he knew about money. He looked like Oscar Homolka as Genghis Khan and trampled over the sensibilities of his Artistic Directors. The very first Council meeting I attended was after the disastrous first night of a play by

Charles Wood, while George was still running the theatre.
'Would you have done this dreadful play?' Neville growled at
me. George had turned his chair away and was sitting in a
corner. 'Certainly,' I lied. He was deeply emotional, vulgar
and a bully but he forced one to define one's own values. He
also relied heavily on the opinion of George Harewood, who
ran the Artistic Committee, a body that originally had to
approve the Director's choice of play. Devine had won his
freedom from that but the committee still existed in a consul-
tative capacity and Harewood could always be relied on in an
emergency to give a clear and dispassionate judgement. I saw
him shield Devine from the attacks of Ronald Duncan and he
supported me through all my crises. At the meeting at which
Neville launched his totally unforeseen attack on me he was
splendid. I never saw him lose his temper and he retained the
friendship and respect of Neville and myself. When it was all
over he showed me the real art of culture politics by rewriting
the wholly accurate minutes of the meeting so that there
would be no record of the true conflict that had taken place.
Neville and I continued to work together, but he was already
in poor health and the relationship was not as warm. When he
died and Harewood left the Council the iron structure that
had held together the organization of the theatre was
weakened. The end of pre-censorship and the declining economic situation played their part. The battles didn't seem so
important any more.

Bond had written his third play, *Narrow Road to the Deep
North*, for a festival organized by Coventry Cathedral, but by
this time I was very tired and I didn't understand the new
play at all. Edward had written it specially for me, knowing
my love of Kurosawa and traditional Japanese theatre, but I
said no and suggested that Jane Howell direct it. The following year we revived all three Bond plays in repertoire in the

main house and even managed to get an enlightened British Council to back a tour of Eastern Europe. The Russians had already taken over in Czechoslovakia; there and in Poland audiences were used to allegorical form concealing political intent and had no trouble in understanding the plays. There were shocked reactions from Embassy staffs to the picture of an England they had never known. 'Why didn't they send us *The Importance of Being Earnest*?' There were questions asked in the Commons and shortly afterwards the Director of the British Council was removed, but we had done it. Bond was a major writer to be reckoned with and his plays were soon being performed by all the leading theatres of Europe.

# 12

# Peter Gill;
# the Lawrence Trilogy

No one quite remembers how Peter Gill arrived in our lives. He was suddenly there like a changeling. Black-haired, skinny, a dock worker's son from Cardiff, he fastened like a succubus on John Dexter and me. He was understudying in *The Long and the Short and the Tall* at the Court and had made friends with Harriet Devine, George's daughter, and moved into that house on Lower Mall that I always think of as ill-fated. George was living with Jocelyn Herbert but would go home there at weekends as a token gesture of something, I'm not sure what. Sophie, his wife, was still devoted to him and had built an extension to the house as a study for him, in the hope of saving the marriage. When I first worked at the Court his life with Jocelyn was a closely kept secret from most of us; he was still preserving the fiction of his marriage. It's difficult to remember how the proprieties had to be maintained in those days, even by the Director of the Royal Court. Sophie was ten years older than George and belonged to his thirties past when Motley, the group of designers to which she belonged, had a studio in St Martin's Lane which was the port of call for Gielgud and his circle. Just as Larry was to marry Joan Plowright as a symbol of a new generation, George found in Jocelyn someone who understood the new work that was being done at the Court. To begin with he did not work with her as a designer perhaps for propriety

or perhaps because she was inexperienced. She had trained
with Margaret Harris and Saint-Denis, but had given it up to
marry and have a family. When the Court started she was a
scene painter on the staff and was first used as a designer by
John Dexter. After the success of *Roots* she became the
Court's unofficial Head of Design and her taste and vision
have dominated the Court's work ever since.

Sophie surrounded herself with a group of young people of
Harriet's generation including Peter Gill, Nicholas Wright
and Michael Fish, who later became a trendy figure in men's
fashion. Sunday lunch was always open house and sometimes
George would turn up and try to teach us to play poker. Peter
and I became very close. He appeared in my production of
*The Chalk Circle* at the Aldwych and shared my excitement
over the rehearsals and the resentment I felt when Peter Hall
took over. He was too highly strung to be a good actor and
wanted to direct. He lived on the edge of danger without
knowing it and was seen everywhere in his winklepicker
shoes. It was not surprising he fell down a waterfall in
Ireland, when on holiday with Sophie and her sister. He
woke in hospital to find himself being given extreme unction.
He was soon back on the scene however. He was with me
when I had the news of my mother's death. It was the cold
winter of 1963 and we had been to see *Lolita* at the Forum,
Fulham Road. I wept in his arms. That summer he came back
to work as my assistant on the production of the Mystery
Plays at the York Festival, and began his career as a director.
He was obsessed by design in the theatre and at the dress
parade was ruthless in his insistence on changes that needed to
be made. To my astonishment he was also quite humourless,
which I now recognize as part of his driving force.

He suffered badly from stomach ulcers. When I took over
the Court in 1965 he joined the staff in the publicity

department. I depended on his advice but wasn't prepared to trust him as a director, though he had already done D. H. Lawrence's *A Collier's Friday Night* as a Sunday night in George's last season. His production of Shaw's *O'Flaherty V.C.* at the Mermaid convinced me of his talent. Bernard Miles said, 'This boy puts pauses into Shaw. It's never been done before.' During my second season he directed *The Soldier's Fortune* and then *The Daughter-in-Law*, which led to the D. H. Lawrence Trilogy in the following year. He obviously had an affinity with the mining background of the three plays. At what point they became fused into a trilogy in his mind, I don't know. His great strength is his ability to take a piece of human activity and focus on it with such care that it acquires a luminous life beyond its function. Some people might call this naturalistic, but it is the antithesis of what is commonly thought of as naturalism and owes very little to Stanislavsky. When I had to take a rehearsal for him when he was ill, I described how I had altered the moment when the mother poured the boiling water on the tea in order to give it time to infuse. He became quite agitated. 'But she must pour it on that line. I've conceived that moment. It would be wrong later.' He was working on a direct intuition of images not unlike Bond.

He also has a boldness with time which is breathtaking but sometimes tends towards mannerism. The most striking example was Luther washing himself when he comes back from the pit in *The Daughter-in-Law*. Lawrence's indications are perfunctory; Luther goes offstage and the dialogue continues with his brother. In Peter's production we could see into the wash-house and the dialogue stopped while Mike Pratt very thoroughly and lovingly washed himself and Victor Henry as Joe nodded in the rocking chair. It must have lasted at least five minutes and we were all spellbound. The ritual of the miner's wash had been stated in *A Collier's Friday Night* when the father was washed by the fire and it came to a great fulfilment in the last play, *The Widowing of Mrs Holroyd*, when the mother and the wife have to wash the dead body of Holroyd on stage. I shall never forget Ann Dyson and Judy Parfitt bent over the body of Michael Coles like a living *pietà* and weeping. The meaning of the three plays was compressed and filled with Peter's own Catholicism. After the run-through of the play I started to give notes to Peter and found myself crying. What else was there to say?

At the dress rehearsal of the first play Peter was rushed to hospital. The ulcer had burst and had to be operated on. Jane Howell and I saw the other two plays through to performance and visited Peter in hospital with progress reports. It was at one of these visits that I let slip that I had changed the timing of the tea business and nearly brought about a relapse. Sometimes he would lie there, still on a saline drip, directing Judy Parfitt at his bedside in whispers so the nurses wouldn't hear. He was let out to see a rehearsal of *Holroyd* but became very worked up in his note session and I had to rush him back to hospital. The plays opened and were a huge success. He had established himself as a director. There was no recurrence of the ulcers but instead the tension he had forced into his stomach became directed to the world outside. From the moment he recovered we were never close again. The energy that had driven him through the work and his illness sealed him off.

It meant, too, that he was not strong enough to share the running of the theatre with me. Desmond's cycles of manic depression had become an embarrassment to me and the theatre. His highs took a very exhibitionist form which included preaching from the pulpit in Westminster Cathedral and giving out daffodils to the actors in the middle of a performance at the RSC, and he had to go. The fights over censorship, with the press and with the Council, had left me exhausted and unsure of what to do next. John Osborne had given us two full-length plays which he called 'For the mean time'. They were both middle-class conversation pieces with little of the passion of his earlier work. *Inadmissible Evidence* was perhaps the last play that spoke with the voice of his generation. The new plays were near West End in feeling; I even met Binkie Beaumont to discuss if he would do them with us. 'Couldn't, my dear. Characters too recognizable. Girl's obviously Vanessa and the dying man, well, it's Godfrey [Tearle], isn't it?' I asked Antony Page to direct them and he cast them up to the hilt with well-known actors including Paul Scofield, making his first appearance at the Court. Both plays transferred and made money for the theatre. The only other transfers prior to this in my regime had been the first plays of Christopher Hampton and David Storey. The money from the Osborne plays financed the season of Bond plays. The theatre had reverted to a pattern of transferring its successes to pay for its experiments.

The end of the Bond season was marked by a drag ball on the stage of the Royal Court. My costume and wig were designed by Deirdre Clancy. I felt I was like Lilian Baylis or Ninette de Valois. I had enormous power without any effort and could have run the place much more easily than as a man. In the middle of the party three black girls appeared as the Supremes linked by yards of orange chiffon. It was Peter Sibley, the Company Manager, Helen Montagu, the General Manager and Jane Howell, who had pretended to be completely uninterested in the whole venture. Ken Cranham won first prize as a rocker in a plastic jacket, mini-skirt and his straight wig in an Alice band.

Perhaps I should have left at this point. A whole cycle of

work had been completed with the end of censorship and the Bond season. The theatre was in a healthy state financially, but the next stage was not clear. I hadn't followed George's advice to his successor, 'Keep your best eye on the horizon, the other on your instruments.' In retrospect the Court's history is marked by the fertile periods of its own writers, of whom there are never more than two or three at any one time, rather than the plans and schemes of its Artistic Director. George's method was to have a stable of five or six writers that he believed in, and about the same number that he wasn't so sure about. I guess I did the same. Both of us misjudged writers, but those we believed in we stuck to. The real trick of the trade is to prepare for the next wave before the current one has spent itself. Writers dry up, have bad periods and nowadays look elsewhere if you don't like their play. At the beginning of the Court's history there was nowhere else. By the time I took over, the RSC had moved to London and the National had opened at the Old Vic. Neither of them had a regular outlet for new work but both had taken risks in the main bill. There was also Michael Codron who had done so much for Pinter, Orton and Charles Wood. A theatre director is also dependent on, and swayed by, the enthusiasm of his associates for particular writers even if he doesn't care for them himself. Dexter's advocacy of Wesker is a case in point. In fact the close ties between writer and director was the most distinguishing feature of the Court's work.

I decided to take time off to work outside Sloane Square and I was under pressure to invite Antony Page to run a season in my absence. Antony, quite reasonably, wanted a share in the running of the theatre on a longer-term basis and this was eventually agreed. He insisted on asking Lindsay to join us so that there was once again a triumvirate. I had never realized how much my old associates had resented not being asked back when I took over, as if they'd been cut out of the family firm. I had asked Lindsay to direct the first David Storey play but he wasn't free. Our relations in the old days under George had been cordial because we all had equal status. But I had been running the theatre autocratically for four years and found it difficult to share power. Our tastes, too, had diverged. Lindsay's heart was back in the old days with its Sunday nights. I had just opened the Theatre Upstairs.

There had always been talk of the Court having its own studio theatre, but for many years the space at the top of the building was Clement Freud's restaurant. When we eventually got rid of him we ran the space as our own club and gradually started doing experimental work. With the end of censorship small club theatres had started to spring up all over London. The first I saw was in Queensway and showed Arden's *Squire Jonathan* in which a girl actually took all her clothes off. The new freedom initially meant bums and tits. Very soon actors were saying and doing things that would have been unthinkable a year before. For a time the upstairs space was a late-night drinking club and plays were performed as a highbrow floor show. I remember sitting with Mick Jagger, drinking champagne and watching a play by Chikamatsu *The Love Suicides in the Women's Temples*. It was like that. Jane Howell, Bill Bryden, Barry Hanson (three of the directors on the staff) and I presented an entirely improvised piece, influenced by the Living Theater, called *A Show of Violence*. I think we kept promising to catch each other when we fell backwards; Bill Bryden kept waving a cudgel within an inch of my ear, and there was a sequence in which we announced our intentions like: 'Bill Gaskill will jump on to a pink chair; Barry Hanson will sit on a black chair.' Of course, drunks in the audience joined in the game: 'Bill Gaskill will go fuck himself.' Like the Living Theater we soon found that only our own anarchy was acceptable; other people's had to be controlled. This period of experiment was happening concurrently with Osborne's rather staid pieces downstairs. It was the kind of theatre he loathes.

After this brief but joyous period of anarchy we decided to convert the space into a full-time theatre, to be run by Nicky Wright, another of my Assistants. It was the first time that the Court had not led the way and it marked a watershed. Anything that was risky or about which one was not absolutely sure could now be sent upstairs. Previously the rigorous demands of the Court's main stage and its 400 seats were an acid test of the viability of a piece, a standard by which new work could be judged. Now it was wide open. Inevitably there was a split in the work. It was not just part of the development of the Royal Court but was experienced in theatres all over the country. The idea of 'alternative theatre' was born.

The divide was even more strongly marked in Sloane Square by the arrival of Lindsay. Although much of his early work had been very experimental, I don't think he has ever liked being a failure at the box office. It's never bothered me. I've thought of my flops as honourable battle scars, though perhaps there have been too many over the years. Lindsay was determined to restore excellence, as he saw it, to the Court on all levels. The three years that followed were marked by his fine productions of David Storey's plays and a succession of star actors. John Gielgud and Ralph Richardson, neither of whom had appeared for the ESC, were bagged in one show, *Home*, and both returned separately, Gielgud in Charles Wood's *Veterans* and Richardson in Osborne's *West of Suez*. I liked the Storey plays though I felt none of them explored the raw passion of his first play, *The Restoration of Arnold Middleton*, or his novel *Radcliffe*. But the precise casting and relaxed ensemble direction of *The Contractor* and *The Changing Room* were in the great Royal Court tradition. I had no big guns of my own till Bond's *Lear* in 1971. I contented myself with directing Howard Barker's first play in the Theatre Upstairs and, with the help of Bill Bryden, preparing a festival of alternative theatre, *Come Together*.

# 13
# Naturalism and
# Images

The division in the work, between the Lawrence plays on the one hand and the new work from America on the other, called in question our values at the Court. The cry, which has been heard from the days of Gordon Craig, was 'Down with naturalism; theatre should be made of images; literary theatre is dead; away with narrative and linear thinking.' But what was naturalism, what were images? Were the new ways of making theatre merely fashionable or did they reflect the times? What place was there for the writer in the work? Plays, as we had always understood them, presented a recognizable society – a society that might be mythical, but which was delineated by a class structure. It was either historical as in *Mother Courage* or imaginary as in *The Chalk Circle*, but it related to a society we knew. As the world of mixed periods started to take over, our grip of what the writer or the group was trying to say became dislocated. We knew they felt strongly; the images disturbed us, as in a dream, but we couldn't always recognize the relevance.

Every action on the stage is in some sense symbolic, from killing a king to pouring a cup of tea. The Lawrence plays, with their detailed observation of working-class life, are the epitome of what would usually be called naturalism but in his productions Peter Gill had shown us the underlying rituals that make up that life. The stage was full of images composed

of the simplest tasks. Is Chardin less of a painter than El
Greco? Many of the Court's plays used a realistic sequence of
people working to create metaphors of society: the waitresses
endlessly circulating round the chefs in *The Kitchen*, the men
putting up the tent in *The Contractor*, the building workers in
*That's Us*. Were these examples of naturalism? The journey
of the cart in *Mother Courage* presents a metaphor for capitalism, but the cart and everything in it are real and have
economic value or there would be no dialectic. If the boots
Courage sells are not real, or if she doesn't actually pull the
cart herself, as I believe happened in the recent RSC production, the metaphor ceases to work. The stage action must
have a realistic logic for its symbols to function and make the
political point. There is nothing surreal about B. B. The cart
may be a symbol of capitalism but it must look real, like all
the stage properties; they are the demonstration of property,
of ownership, just as the baby in *The Chalk Circle* is property,
which belongs to Grusche because she looks after it better
than its real mother.

The robing of the Pope in *Galileo* is also symbolic. In the
scene the Pope is first seen in his underwear, humane and
liberal. By the time he is fully robed he has agreed to Galileo
being shown the instruments of torture. But in real life popes
are robed with ceremony – perhaps not as elaborately as in
the Berliner Ensemble's production – and the scene exists on
a perfectly realistic level. When Pip, the rebel in Wesker's
*Chips with Everything*, puts on the officer's uniform and joins
the Establishment, the dressing is insufficiently motivated in
the scene. The image becomes detached from its realistic base
and is seen nakedly as the writer's statement.

In the last scene but one of *Saved* the father comes to visit
Len, who is lying on the floor with a knife in his hand,
clearing a crack in the floorboards so he can hear whether

Pam is with her lover. The father has been hit over the head with a teapot in the previous scene and has a bandage round his head; he is about to go to bed and is dressed in his combinations and socks. Perhaps the image that Edward had in mind was of a ghost, and a suicide figure on the floor, like a Victorian problem picture. He insisted that Harry's socks should be white too, to create this image, as if it were in a dream. Nothing in the scene is unexplained in realistic terms, but the need for the picture precedes the scene. The end of the play when Len mends the chair has been taken by *raisonneurs*, at the author's own evaluation, as a symbol of optimism. Edward admitted that the images were drawn from attitudes of *grief* in classical statuary and certainly the last moment is one of repose or acceptance, with Len's head lying on the seat, his right hand dangling as he becomes part of the death around him. This is the image the writer has created and no special pleading, Marxist or otherwise, will alter it. It had a strange memory for me of the end of *George Dillon* where George is also absorbed into the life-in-death of the family he detests.

In *Early Morning* we entered the dream world itself, in which the intellectual meaning of the play starts to be verbalized and even some of the symbols explained, as if Bond couldn't trust them to work by themselves. The Brechtian world of reality, where people are hungry, need to sell boots to live and where the moral values are clear is left behind. The father in *Saved* looked like a ghost, in *Early Morning* Prince Albert is a ghost. By the time Bond wrote *Lear* the ghost of the Gravedigger's Boy had become a central figure in the action. Does this movement towards a dream world mean an inability to face the reality of the society in which we live? In fact, Bond has become more politically dogmatic as the plays have less of the detail of contemporary life. He needs to express his ideas through imagery rather than observation. It's difficult to find this dislocation theatrically expressive.

It's also hard for actors to play symbols with which they can't identify. In Stanislavsky the actor says, 'I might behave like that'; in Brecht he says, 'Look at the way he behaves'; with Bond he is trying to fulfil an image that has no rational connection to human behaviour, an image in the writer's mind. It's true that actors' ideas of human behaviour are limited. How often do you hear an actor say, 'My character wouldn't do that,' meaning, 'I can't imagine my character doing that.' Like Brack at the end of *Hedda Gabler* they say, 'People don't do that sort of thing,' when Hedda, whether they like it or not, has shot herself. Every director and every writer has been impatient of this attitude. It indicates a limited awareness of human potential. But to deny any coherent pattern to human behaviour is also limiting and denies the actors any sense of belonging to the play's development. They are like characters in *Tom and Jerry* flattened against a wall and disintegrating in a pile of bricks one minute, but, in the next frame, alive and well; the creation of the cartoonist's brush. Of course, actors will bring their own feelings and experience of reality to any text – Gielgud in *No Man's Land* for example – but it can be a sterile task. I feel puzzled by this trend in theatre today – not just in the work of Bond. I'm out of sympathy with the rejection of humanism, which is made philosophically and theatrically, and can't help actors to present it. Artaud was never an influence on me and I found much of the Theatre of Cruelty modish rather than searching. There is also a strange ambiguity in the presentation of violence that I mistrust in myself as well as in the work of others. When Fortinbras enters at the end of *Hamlet* in black leather and, instead of restoring sanity to the state of Denmark, shoots Horatio and establishes a Fascist state, I wonder if this isn't what Ingmar Bergman wants to happen; just as much a wish-fulfilment as Shakespeare's dream of order returning to the body politic. From Orton onwards we have lived through a re-creation of the theatre of the Weimar Republic, clown faces, transvestism, left-wing politics and a kind of hysteria which no doubt reflects the swing to the right in Europe. The bright-eyed idealism of the early Wesker plays and the Aldermaston March may no longer be possible, but I cannot believe in the politics or the art that has replaced it. It is too like an imitation of the past.

# 14

# The American Influence;
# Bond's *Lear*

By 1970 nearly all the major American groups had visited London. At the Court we had been host to the Bread and Puppet Theater, La Mama under Andres Serban and a late-night production of Michael McLure's *The Beard*, which is an imaginary dialogue between Jean Harlow and Billy the Kid. At the end of the play Billy goes down on Jean Harlow and as he puts his tongue in the 'Hallelujah Chorus' bursts forth and the night sky is filled with stars. Or so we were supposed to believe. One night as the lights faded the voice of Billie Dixon who played Harlow could be heard: 'I told you not to do that.' She did in fact wear a G-string. She was entertaining in her dressing room after the show when the stage manager came in with a fresh G-string for the following night. 'How could you do that in front of members of the public?' said Billie. 'I'm not supposed to wear anything. You've ruined the illusion.' 'Oh, we don't believe in illusion here. This is the Royal Court.'

The greatest revelation was the Bread and Puppet Theater, under the direction of Peter Schuman. Some of their plays were simple parables performed outside in Sloane Square, some were projections of the Bible. All used the most beautiful masks I've ever seen. I often wonder what George would have made of it; a work so far beyond anything that he or Saint-Denis could have dreamed of, completely outside the

literary tradition of the Court. They invaded our con-
sciousness as powerfully as the Berliner Ensemble twelve
years before.

The creation of the Fringe in those years was the work of
Americans, Jim Haynes at the Arts Lab, Charles Marowitz at
the Open Space, Ed Berman with Inter-Action and Nancy
Meckler at the Freehold. Soon there were groups everywhere
and I decided to organize a huge festival at the Court, which
we called *Come Together*. Christopher Hampton's play *The
Philanthropist* was steadily earning money in the West End so
we could afford to lose our shirt. The battered old building in
Sloane Square seemed a really unsuitable venue (as theatres
came to be called, just as performances were now called gigs).
Peter Cheeseman from Stoke needed a theatre-in-the-round
for his company, some of the performance artists (another
new term) needed a completely free space, and Bill Bryden
was already arranging rock bands at knock-down prices. The
Court with its proscenium, circle and gallery couldn't have
been more intractable.

Hayden Griffin set about reconstructing the theatre. The
stalls were removed and a new stage built above the existing
stage, projecting into the auditorium, high enough for the
public in the circle to see. A new bank of seats was built at the
back of the stage so that the circle audience was looking at a
mirror image of itself. This went some way towards theatre-
in-the-round. The stalls were a promenade, though most of
the audience chose to sit on the floor. The whole theatre was
painted in primary colours by Di Seymour. There were
usually two shows a night in the main theatre and one in the
Theatre Upstairs.

The festival opened with a new piece from The People
Show, the only group surviving from that period today. I
recall only a succession of images, a live rabbit tethered to a

chair panicking and knocking over a pot of red paint on the new stage cloth (I was told this was unintentional) and at the end the audience being driven out with ear-piercing music and smoke and the group throwing oranges at the critics. It wasn't one of their best pieces. One they did later with Laura Gilbert riding round naked on a tricycle and a great hopper of newspaper cascading over the stage was much better. In his piece *Foul Fowl* Peter Dockley filled the stage with hens in chicken coops and relayed their clucking throughout the theatre. It even came over the Tannoy in Helen Montagu's office. Helen happens to be phobic about birds. At some point foam spread insidiously across the stage and the clucking got worse.

The most violent piece was Stuart Brisley's, which consisted of him steadily eating bread and drinking water as 'God Save the Queen' was played forwards and backwards until he finally climbed a scaffolding tower and was sick. We had gone too far for Jocelyn Herbert and the old guard. Only Oscar Lewenstein was determinedly with it. The Court's contribution was my Beckett plays in the Theatre Upstairs, and Heathcote Williams's *AC/DC*, the most avant-garde of all Court plays. Originally called *Skizotopia* it ended with Victor Henry being trepanned to open up what, I believe, is called the third eye. Oh, my Leary and my Ginsberg long ago.

Lindsay had watched this counter-culture sweep through the Court, unmoved. He probably knew it would not seriously change the work of the Court, and indeed it didn't. None of the groups needed the theatre in the way that the early writers had needed the Court. In fact we needed them, our monkey glands against the hardening of the arteries. It frustrated me that so much creative energy was being poured into work outside the Court tradition. In the following year I returned to my Epic masters, Brecht with *Man is Man* ( a not very good production of an unsatisfactory play) and Bond with his new play *Lear*.

In retrospect it's clear that Edward had embarked on a path in which he would challenge the cultural archetypes of Western civilization: Shakespeare, and the Greeks. *Early Morning* had been his problem play, about a Hamlet figure who stands outside society, obsessed with its suffering, without being capable of changing it. Unlike Hamlet, however, it is not clear till halfway through the play that Arthur is the central figure. By calling his central character Lear, Bond forced himself and us to acknowledge where the focus of the play lay. In the process he challenged comparison not only with Shakespeare's quality as a writer, but with his control of narrative and his development of the action. In Shakespeare everything is set in motion by Lear's actions in the first scene, 'The bow is bent and drawn; make from the shaft'; the play unrolls its length dynamically from that moment. In the beginning of Bond's play Lear is also violent and irrational: he shoots an innocent workman to expedite the building of the symbolic wall which is to protect him against his enemies. It triggers the civil war between him and his daughters but it does not set in motion the rest of the play. Perhaps no play written today can contain that kind of energy. No one quite believes in cause and effect, or the power of the individual to dominate action, as Renaissance writers did. Bond's plays seem to stop and start; they don't flow inexorably onwards. It is partly a Brechtian technique of preventing the spectator from getting caught up in the action but more often mirrors Bond's need to stop to define his own moral attitudes. In his work he has moved from the no-metaphor, no-explanation theory – that he would have shared with Keith Johnstone and Ann Jellicoe in the early days – to making political or philosophical statements, which exist side by side with his poetic images. And with his need to explain himself, his prefaces have become longer. His work, which could not have been more anti-Shavian, has ended up not unlike Shaw.

Again the play was in three massive acts, and again there was a distinct sensation of the play starting all over again in Act Three. In all Bond's work there is a constant search by the central character – and one imagines by the author – to find the right moral action. As Grusche says in *The Chalk Circle*, 'Great is the temptation of goodness.' Lear's move towards moral responsibility is shown in his relation with the Gravedigger's Boy, who is killed in Act One and returns as a ghost in Act Two. The Ghost represents Lear's desire to escape from identification with suffering humanity and the responsibilities that go with it. As long as the Ghost is there like a succubus Lear is avoiding the action he must take. When he decides to act the Ghost dies. (How can a ghost die? Don't ask me.) The action to which the whole play has led is his attempt to dig up the wall, and he is shot. In some ways the action is as ineffectual as Len's mending of the chair in *Saved*. (Len is another inadequate seeker after goodness.) Both actions are existential: they may not change the world but they have to be done. Since then Edward has attempted to conform to a Marxist concept of action and tries to reinterpret his earlier work by claiming a more positive political intent. (Though he has always said that the end of *Saved* was optimistic in spite of its images of grief.)

The play is on a huge scale and even with intensive doubling needed a cast of twenty-five. Finding a Lear was not easy. The play has more unremitting violence than any of Bond's plays. Lear, not Gloucester, has his eyes removed in a clinical operation and has to examine the entrails of his dead daughter – a physical realization of Shakespeare's 'Then let them anatomize Regan, see what breeds about her heart.' This was too much for Gielgud, to whom I sent the play. He was also concerned with Bond's quirky inconsistencies: 'Why is she called Cordelia when she isn't his daughter and why is one of them called Cornwall and the other isn't Albany and . . . Oh no, I couldn't fish out the entrails. Better get someone else.' The someone else was Harry Andrews, who I don't think understood the play at all, but whose craggy presence gave us a strong centre. The rest of the play was cast with some of the most imaginative of the younger actors around at the time including Bob Hoskins, the only actor in the world who could keep his sense of humour while kicking someone in the teeth, while Rosemary McHale as Fontanelle screeched, 'Let me sit on his lungs.' This was a scene I particularly hated directing; it's when you catch yourself saying, 'When you push the needles in his ears could you just be a little more ironical on the doo–dee–doo–dee–doo' that you realize you're in danger of joining the band of sadists yourself.

John Napier designed the set and Deirdre Clancy the costumes. Again Deirdre did some pre-rehearsal sketches of the play which established the character of the production. Bond is deliberately vague about the period of the play and would not give us a lead, apart from saying Lear should look like Leonardo da Vinci. We toyed with ancient Britons and then Renaissance. The deciding factor was the rifles. It's funny how means of killing people dictate a period. *Hamlet* and *Twelfth Night* both have key scenes involving duelling with swords and therefore belong in a world before 1914. Rifles cannot be pre-nineteenth century. Rifles meant uniforms, and gradually a look emerged which had a Russian character of about 1900. In the first act Lear wore a white greatcoat and in the last, when he has become a pacifist prophet, looked like Tolstoy in his *moujik* outfit. The underbelly of the play started to show itself. The Tsarist state is overthrown in a palace revolution, which in turn is overthrown by a people's party. By the last act this has become a Stalinist government led by Cordelia, a Thatcherite figure married to the silent carpenter of Act One. In Deirdre's original drawing he is in a suit but we changed it to a uniform and in it Oliver Cotton looked very like Stalin. None of this was our original intention; we were fulfilling Edward's anachronistic dream world as best we could. In the process a political slant was revealed without being stressed. Unlike Brecht, who creates a mythical fairy-tale world to draw a political parallel, Bond makes a dream world in which the reality of rifles jostles a Shakespearian myth. The poet and the political thinker are trying to co-exist, a struggle that has gone on in Bond ever since. But the play, as far as it is polemical at all, is pacifist, against violence, and sceptical of political change by the masses. It is finally the action of one man that counts.

Napier's set used the Court stage brilliantly. The wall that dominates the play was not seen at all till the very last scene. In the early scenes it was imagined by the actors to be out front. During the rest of the play its enormous structure in two sections was housed behind the side panels of the surround. In the blackout before the last scene the panels flew up and the halves locked into place. When the lights came up this massive structure towered over the audience. Edward had, as usual, a great instinct about this. He also suggested that the two prison scenes should be quite different: one should have a solid three-sided wall, confining the acting area, the other could use the whole stage space. A year after the London production I redirected the play at the Munich State Theatre on a stage twice the size; afterwards it was difficult to believe we had ever been able to get it on the Court stage, but our achievement is that we did. It was perhaps the last of the

Court's epic productions in all senses of the word.

The play was more respectfully received than Bond's previous work, apart from an attack from the Minister for the Arts, who said it was exactly the kind of play on which public money should not be spent. It played to about 60 per cent business and was immediately bought by most of the leading theatres in Germany. While I was directing *Lear* in Munich Edward was making his début as a director at the Burg Theater in Vienna with the same play. They were trying to rejuvenate that most traditional of all state theatres by importing the avant-garde talent of Great Britain. Bond's first real success had been with Peter Stein's production of *Saved* at the Kammerspiele in Munich and by this time his plays were in demand all over Europe, or more exactly northern Europe. It's a depressing fact that the violence that had prevented the success of his plays in England seemed to make him more acceptable in Germany. In Munich the audience sat calmly through the death of the Boy behind the washing line, the rape of the pregnant woman, the kicking and the ear-puncturing and the evisceration of Fontanelle. But when the doctor began the blinding of Lear and said, 'This isn't an instrument of torture but a scientific device,' and the eyes (two large grapes) went plop, plop into the formaldehyde it was too much for the Bavarian bourgeoisie. '*Aufhören, aufhören, Schweinerei*,' they shouted. Culture could be gloomy and satisfy their *Weldschmerz* but this was too reminiscent of Dachau.

Bodice, the elder sister, was to have been played by Hanne Hiob, Brecht's daughter by his first wife. She is a remarkable actress and was going to be very striking in the part. Unfortunately in the middle of rehearsal I gave an interview to the local press and was quoted as saying that the play was an attack on the Russian Revolution. Hanne immediately left the cast. 'I cannot be in a play which my father would not have approved of.' I tried to persuade her of my left-wing credentials and devotion to her father and Edward Bond sent a marvellous cake from Demel's, the bakery in Vienna, iced with a picture of Lenin, but it was no use.

*Lear* was Bond's last play that I was to direct while running the Court and it seemed to have exhausted his extreme violence. His next play *The Sea* (1973) is his most benign. The only violence is the stabbing of the dead body by Hatch, the draper – played by Ian Holm. For the first time there is a romantic relation between two young people and though the matriarch Mrs Rafi is in a sense a descendant of Queen Victoria, the mother ogress, she is much more benevolent. It is Bond's *Tempest* and like that play it completed a cycle of work. I returned to direct it in 1973 when Oscar Lewenstein was in charge of the theatre. To date it is the last of his plays that I have directed.

Having written *King Lear* and *The Tempest* Bond tackled Shakespeare himself in *Bingo*, the play he wrote for Jane Howell at the Northcott Theatre in Exeter. In it he is very aware of the autobiographical cycle of his own work: 'I stilled the storm in myself,' he makes Shakespeare say. Both this play and *The Fool* that followed it are about writers and their relation to the violence of the world in which they live; Shakespeare, the bourgeois, and John Clare, the working-class poet. It's difficult not to see these as self-portraits. Like Shakespeare, Edward sits in his garden at Great Wilbraham, with an old gardener and his wife – even if he is not making deals to enclose common land – and he certainly sees himself as Clare, the uneducated artist. The poet observer is an extension of Len in *Saved* who watches the baby-stoning without taking part ('Wass it feel like when yer killed it?') and of Arthur in *Early Morning* ('I'm a limited person. I can't face another hungry child, a man with one leg . . .').

It's difficult to explain why it was that I didn't continue to direct Bond's plays. I was offered *The Fool* and turned it down. I couldn't follow the path that Bond was set on. I wasn't even sure what it was. The images in the plays had become icons of inhumanity and suffering that failed to touch me. The crucified vagrant in *Bingo*, a re-creation of a Rembrandt, is static and part of a schema; in *The Fool* when the character cries persistently while the Parson is stripped I feel as if I'm being manipulated. I don't know why the man goes on crying except that Bond wants that particular effect, or why there is the offstage laughter in the prison scene. My withers are unwrung. At the same time a reach-me-down Marxism is being spelt out. Bond seems determined to follow all the way in the footsteps of B.B. and impose a dialectical theory on his imagination. The difference is that B.B. was more naturally a poet than Bond and his Marxism was adopted in Germany at a time when it would have been impossible to take any other course. No doubt Bond would say that England today is in just such another crisis, with Thatcher in the role of Hitler, but I think that is too simplistic. Most of all his politicization has meant the disappearance of the psychological detail and of the humour that were so characteristic of his earlier work. The plays have become gloomier and more pompous and he has deliberately stopped writing about contemporary life in any direct way.

# 15

# The New Writers;
# Departure

While I was struggling with *Lear* in 1971 a group of writers
were meeting to voice their dissatisfaction with the Court and
the opportunities it gave to writers. Among them was David
Hare, who had been Literary Manager and then Resident
Dramatist in succession to Christopher Hampton. In George
Devine's time there was no official Literary Manager, though
Keith Johnstone was paid a miserable pittance to look after
the scripts and all the dramatists were resident. It would have
been invidious to single one out. When I took over in 1965 –
under the influence of my time at the National – I appointed a
Literary Manager but there was still no Resident Dramatist.
Edward Bond was firmly attached to the theatre for over
three years and was much closer to fulfilling that title than
most incumbents, even though he was already living in Cam-
bridgeshire. In 1968 Margaret Ramsay, the writers' agent,
sent me a copy of a play by an Oxford undergraduate with a
firm injunction that it must be read at once and Peggy Ramsay is She Who Must be Obeyed. It was Hampton's first play,
*When Did You Last See My Mother?*. I read it straightaway and
liked it, one of the most attractive first plays I'd ever read. It
was in every sense a post-Osborne play in the sureness of its
invective and emotional warmth. Christopher was eighteen
when he wrote it, which is now rather ordinary when there
are schoolgirls of ten having plays produced, but then it was

remarkable. Bob Kidd, one of my Assistants, seized upon it and scheduled it for a Sunday night, with Victor Henry in the lead. He directed all Hampton's plays till his death in 1980, one of the two pugnacious Scots on the directing staff (the other was Bill Bryden). Victor was also to play Rimbaud in *Total Eclipse* which Christopher wrote for us while he was still a pupil of Enid Starkie at Oxford. I was having a drink with Christopher in the Theatre Upstairs when he was about to do his finals. 'Why not come and join us?' I said on the spur of the moment. We scraped a salary together and he was installed as Resident Dramatist and Literary Manager. It was the first time we'd had someone who could read both French and German on the staff. To quote Devine on Osborne, 'He always was a natty dresser,' and still is. I remember him with his soft Cavalier hair and suits of pale beige. I was going to direct his third play, *The Philanthropist*, but I was going through a very confused period in my life and opted to do Howard Barker's first play, *Cheek*, instead. Bob Kidd's production was enormously successful and ran at the Mayfair for nearly three years. It made a lot of money for all of us and made the *Come Together* festival possible.

Christopher had been at school with David Hare and suggested he should take over the Script Department and David became Resident Dramatist when Christopher left. The class background of these new writers was not in the cosmology we had known when the Court started. Unlike early Court writers they were public-school boys and had been to the older universities, though without the imperial background of Lindsay and Antony. The staff directors, Bob Kidd, Bill Bryden (from Scotland) and Barry Hanson and Pam Brighton (from Bradford), had some of the working-class ambition of their predecessors, Peter Gill and John Dexter, but it was levelling out. Though David Hare was the

Resident Dramatist he never acquired a director on the staff who would fight for his plays. He'd already run his own theatre group, Portable Theatre, with Snoo Wilson and didn't accept the Court tradition at all. Howard Brenton was the other writer whose plays were being presented in the Theatre Upstairs but his first work had been done at the Brighton Combination. Neither he nor Hare belonged to the Court in the same way as earlier writers. When they met in joint protest, with four other writers, they decided to write a play together there and then on rolls of old wallpaper. The result was called *Lay-By* and might have been written especially to provoke Lindsay's contempt. 'Are you responsible for this?' he whispered audibly to Christopher at a reading of the play. I was too involved with *Lear* to realize that it marked a division between the writers and directors in the theatre which was not healthy. I found Lindsay's attitude reactionary but I didn't like the play much either.

Howard Barker wasn't really a child of the Court, though I directed his first play, *Cheek*, in 1970. Like Bond's early work it is personal and intimate. If it has a political message, it isn't clear. I probably responded to it because it reminded me of early Bond, and I cast two actors, Ken Cranham and Tom Chadbon, who had played in the Bond season. The very title of Barker's next play, *No One Was Saved*, challenged Bond's optimism, and introduced actual characters from the earlier play. Although he and Bond have diverged politically Barker still echoes many of Bond's images. The building of the castle in Barker's recent play has the same symbolic power as the building of the wall in Bond's *Lear*; there is a decaying body attached to the witch in *The Castle*, like the skeleton to Arthur in *Early Morning*. At one time Howard would have unquestionably been a Court writer, championed over a number of years. But even if I'd stayed at the Court I don't know that I would have taken him on. It would have involved me in the same kind of difficult relationship with a sombre and individual imagination that I'd had with Bond. You need a lot of commitment for that. He became typical of the rootless writer of today. Plays commissioned by the National end up at the RSC and vice versa, and if the Court turns a play down it will be done elsewhere. This ought to be healthy but in practice it means there is no real critical dialogue between writer and theatre. Such a dialogue has never been easy. The Court's tradition was to protect writers from commercial pressures. In the process writers have been spoiled, have been sheltered from the responsibility of communicating with an audience or have become dishonest about what that would mean. Bond once said he wrote his plays for the people of Southend. He doesn't answer the question, 'Why aren't they done there?' Barker has faced the reality of the limited audience who see his plays and takes pride in being élitist. I find both positions arrogant but I understand how circumstances have dictated them.

Has the Court failed by not providing the theatre in which Arden, Bond and Barker could have gone on developing? I doubt it could ever have worked. They demand a political and poetic exclusivity which it is impossible to meet. Their plays, like most of the Court's experiments, emptied the house and were paid for by the work of Osborne and Hampton, whom they would dismiss as bourgeois, as much as by the Arts Council subsidy. The first years of the Court were carried entirely by the transfers and film rights of Osborne's plays. Soon after I took over in 1965 the Arts Council grant was doubled and I managed without transfers for over three years. Later we were dependent on one play, Hampton's *The Philanthropist*, to finance our risks. This equation has dominated the Court's history. It was never cynical. Osborne and

Hampton are both fine writers and their plays were once risks, too. But each new writer makes new demands on a theatre and its audiences. Bond became accepted by a minority audience after an about-turn by the critics, and so was Barker after a persistent struggle and a continuous output of not less than one play a year. But their determination to go on working for the theatre as a medium is remarkable.

David Hare's commissioned play, *The Great Exhibition*, was disappointing. I wanted desperately to like it enough to do it myself – after all, he was our writer – but I didn't and obviously neither Lindsay nor Antony would do it. It ended up at Hampstead directed by Richard Eyre. The new generation of writers felt understandably rejected in the theatre they felt by right was theirs. I don't know how much of this I was aware of at the time. The theatre was riding the crest of a wave. Plays by Osborne, Bond and Storey followed each other in the autumn of 1971, all expensive with huge casts, and the year ended with the best box-office figures in its history. My dissatisfaction had been growing as much with myself as with the tussles with Lindsay and Antony. I couldn't fight their programme suggestions with new plays that I believed in. My last attempt was Harold Mueller's *Big Wolf*, a play about a group of boys roaming the countryside after the war, which I think one of my best productions. We rehearsed it in freezing cold warehouses filled with rubble. It emptied the house. It was time to go. Oscar Lewenstein, who had been the General Manager when I first joined the Court, had been biding his time. He took over the Chairmanship of the Board when Neville Blond died and suggested he should be the new Artistic Director with the three of us as Associates if we wished. The others said yes. I had a last attempt to rethink the possibility of my starting again single-handed, but it could not have worked. I'd been there seven years.

# 16

# Summing Up;
# Joint Stock

In Edward Bond's next play, *Bingo*, Shakespeare sits in his garden in New Close and asks repeatedly, 'Was anything done?' After running the Royal Court for seven years it was difficult not to do the same. The need to provide a continuous programme of new writing for two theatres and satisfy a 60 per cent box office of the 400 seats in the main house had eroded many of my original aims. Like George Devine I still nursed dreams of what the Court might have: a permanent group of actors, a studio attached to the theatre exploring new ways of working and a committed but popular audience. The ensemble of my first season had folded and though we had returned to groups of actors for the Bond and the Lawrence seasons we could no longer afford a full-scale company on regular salary. The studio work disappeared because we were all too busy running the theatre and directing plays to teach. Even in the first season the existence of a company created for the three opening plays started to dictate the repertoire. I directed a classic – *A Chaste Maid in Cheapside* – to satisfy my company of twenty-five actors. I was in danger of running a theatre for the sake of the actors and directors and not for the writers; at the Court it must obviously be for the latter. There was also pressure from writers to have their plays cast with the best possible actors and for the future exploitation of their work in the West End and on Broadway, though Bond, for example, made a very adequate living from his plays being presented in the subsidized state theatres of Germany.

It was difficult to argue the case for an alternative to the great successes of the star productions of the early seventies. With one or two exceptions, such as *The Changing Room*, the only shows that had filled the theatre were those with one or more of the actor knights or Paul Scofield. This was exactly as it had been in George Devine's time and should have surprised nobody. It was very easy to see the Court as an up-market non-commercial management doing new plays with the strongest possible casts. What was wrong with that? I was still dissatisfied. I knew that it was important to look ahead, to the new generation of writers and actors. I think all the good work of the Court has come from a group of people who for a time have shared the same aims and to some extent tastes. I don't think these groups would have come into being if Devine had not originally conceived an ensemble in which this could happen. In retrospect the fact that the acting companies with which he and I both started our regimes at the Court didn't outlast the first season is not important. They gave the theatre a centre and laid the foundations for future seasons. The strong ties that developed between writers and directors and between directors and designers as well as the continuing use of the same actors gave the work an identity it would not otherwise have had. For me the Court's best work was when these connections were strongest: the Wesker/Dexter/Jocelyn Herbert productions; Peter Gill's work on the D. H. Lawrence plays with John Gunter and Deirdre Clancy; Lindsay Anderson and David Storey, with Gunter and Jocelyn Herbert; the Bond season with Gunter, Clancy and Hayden Griffin. And, of course, the work of Andy Phillips, who had designed the lighting for nearly all the productions during my time.

If I don't mention the actors it is because there were so many who brought their own freshness and individuality to the complex demands of the writing. The skills of actors have developed unbelievably since my days in weekly rep. They have had to follow the demands of the writer. They have put up a marquee in *The Contractor*, mixed cement in *That's Us*, played rugby with David Storey, and pretended to eat human flesh for Edward Bond. Nothing has fazed them. And from the writer's words they have found new ways of speaking. The floating population of enormous talent finding work where it can and moving between classics and new work, between stage and television and films, between fringe theatres and the large subsidized houses, is the glory of our theatre. It does mean we can never have the rich character-acting in small parts that is so satisfying in the state ensembles of the Continent, but we have a reservoir of actors of great range and flexibility.

The studio that I'd started at the Court in 1963 survived for three years under Keith Johnstone's direction and there were sporadic revivals of it when the Theatre Upstairs started, but it became detached from the group of the main house and never developed a theatre piece for it. Keith's group, Theatre Machine, was a direct product of the studio's first term, in which we concentrated on improvised comedy, but it was not based in Sloane Square. The failure to keep the studio going meant that I had not found the time to recharge my batteries and develop new approaches to directing. All theatre directors dream of this but few succeed in making it a reality. Once you run a theatre it takes over not just in the plays you have to direct but in the day-to-day running of the building itself. Peter Brook has always realized this and kept himself free to take his time on each project. Joan Littlewood almost brought it off by a combination of flair and bloody-mindedness, but it's not easy.

My other major frustration at the time I left was our inability to find any kind of regular audience in Sloane Square. Our successes were West End successes and drew a West End audience. Our failures, like *Big Wolf*, emptied the house. It's not enough that years later someone – a young actor or university student – will tell you how remarkable it was. You need an audience then and there, even if it's a minority audience. One play – *Life Price* – was so appallingly received that the houses were too small for us to continue playing. I decided to open the theatre free to anyone who wanted to come. Doubters said it wouldn't work but it did. The theatre was packed with people, many of whom were not regular theatre-goers. You could tell that by the beer bottles they took in with them. I don't know whether it could have been repeated but I was uplifted by the experience and even started to budget for a completely free theatre. It was a Utopian dream and the profit-and-loss boys sent out warning signals, particularly the Arts Council. When they talk so disgustingly about 'bums on seats' – which they do – they always mean paying bums on seats.

During my last year or so at the Court I became friendly with Max Stafford-Clark, who had brought his group from the Traverse Theatre in Edinburgh to the Theatre Upstairs. Max is about ten years younger than me, from a generation more interested in pop music and football than Shakespeare and classical ballet. He had spent a year in New York working at La Mama and absorbed some of what Ellen Stewart calls 'the search for the psychic orgasm'. He, too, had had enough of running an organization and was about to give it up. One day, about a year or so after we had both become free, we started talking about methods of work and what we felt like doing next. Out of this grew our collaboration in the Joint Stock Theatre Group, founded by Max, David Hare and David Aukin, for what purpose no one was quite sure but Max kept calling it 'an umbrella organization'. It looked as if it might keep the rain off Max Stafford-Clark.

In our first Joint Stock workshop (another new term that replaced the 'studios' of the fifties) on Heathcote Williams's book *The Speakers* we explored all the areas that had been impossible while running a theatre: working with a group of actors without a deadline, sharing ideas and exercises. Max taught me the trust exercises he had learned at La Mama and I taught him something of what I had learned about writing. Heathcote was not involved in the making of the play from his book. For me, perhaps more than for Max, it was important to feel some freedom from the presence of the writer and the discipline of the finished text. Max and I made the script ourselves using dialogue from the book, which was largely actual conversations and speeches recorded by Heathcote at the time he knew the speakers in Hyde Park.

The success of *The Speakers* launched us on our next project, *Fanshen*, adapted from William Hinton's book about a village in revolutionary China. This time we asked David Hare to write the play and he became part of the initial workshop, which involved most of the actors from *The Speakers*. We had already developed a working method which became known as the Joint Stock process: a workshop in which the material was explored, researched and improvised around, a gap in which the writer went away and wrote the play, and an extended rehearsal period of a more conventional kind. From the beginning David had a very firm sense of the structure of the book and perhaps of the eventual play. It's a long book full of detail and we were talking of a cast of nine. The workshop was run on democratic lines of group discussion and self-examination, mirroring the movement of the villagers in the book towards socialism. As we explored the growth of their knowledge and understanding our own awareness of group responsibility developed. Hare's play caught this experience in a spare and penetrating piece of work. The essential difference between this process and the work of nearly all other groups is that the writer maintains his control and authority over the material, even though the rest of the group has fed ideas, attitudes and characterization into it. In the rehearsal period the text is treated with the same respect as any new play, though the actors discuss it more freely and know the background more fully than they ever would in a Bond play, for example, where the actor is entering the private world of the writer. *Fanshen* was a public play in which none of the ideas was private; everything could be debated. For me it was a fulfilment of the process started on *The Chalk Circle* and thwarted by the demands of the RSC and Peter Hall, the process in which the actors share an understanding of the political responsibility of the play; they are not just there to serve the writer but, together with the writer, are making a statement.

Edward Bond called Joint Stock 'the Royal Court in exile', though he has never written for the group and would find it difficult. In a sense it was a just description. I had brought from the Court to the Fringe a respect for the text which Max had responded to and the marriage of our separate experience of theatre had produced the Joint Stock method. It has been difficult to maintain. The group was never really political in any doctrinaire way, though it has tended to deal with socially relevant subjects. Caryl Churchill is the only writer who has gone through the process more than once. Writers need to return to the world of their own imagination and feel exposed in the group process; good writers, that is; there are always some who will settle for journalism rather than poetry. But the body of work produced has been impressive.

I feel that it achieved the dream of the committed ensemble, the true balance of writer, director and actors.

So much of directing is responding to the imagination of the writer and translating it for the actors. Sometimes the demands of the writer seem exorbitant or take you outside what you think to be truly theatrical. But from my first experience of N. F. Simpson's timing, I have been amazed at the writer's understanding of what theatre could be, rather than what it is. At the same time I have tried to keep a weather eye on their divergence from what I consider to be basic theatrical values. Too many writers today are writing plays in the form of film or television scripts, involving the director in massive scene changes. Epic has come to mean big stages with huge trucks trundling on and off bearing entire rooms. When they judder to a halt the scene that follows is often domestic or argumentative and has acquired epic grandeur only by the use of a piece of machinery. It has not fulfilled the real experience of theatre. 'A theatre stage should have the maximum of verbal presence and the maximum of corporal presence.'

When Irving Wardle asked me about my policy at the Court I am said to have replied, 'Policy is the people you work with,' and in a way I meant it. But even having committed yourself to particular writers you are dependent on their productivity and their development and on your own continuing identity with what they are trying to say, even if that could be defined. Some of the writers I was closest to, like Simpson and Jellicoe, dried up; Wally had shot like a comet across our sky and could not sustain his brilliance, Ann herself has said that having children replaced her need to write. Arden always had anarchic leanings, encouraged by his wife, and started to work outside the mainstream in near-amateur conditions. I have a feeling that even if his plays had been a success inside the establishment, at some point he would have wanted to kick against it. When their play *The Island of the Mighty* was done at the RSC he and Margaretta D'Arcy climbed on the stage to pull down the scenery in protest at what they felt was a distortion of their work. But for a time it had looked as if he was our Brecht.

Wesker has gone on writing but his plays have been ignored by the major companies. He is convinced that this is some deep-laid conspiracy in the Establishment to prevent his work reaching the stage – Arden thinks this is so about his work, but for political reasons. I don't think Wesker can face the fact that his early autobiographical plays had an immediacy his later work lacks.

I've always sought those writers whose work I could identify with and I was lucky to find, even for a brief period, a writer like Edward Bond of whom that was true. Even with Bond I only felt that absolute certainty with *Saved* and started to diverge from him in his later plays. Perhaps this was also connected with Edward's increasing need to have a more direct control over the production. When I turned down *The Fool* in 1975 it was directed by Peter Gill, himself a writer, who has his own personal use of theatre imagery and was bound to conflict with Bond. Ever since, with the exception of *Bingo* and *The Bundle*, Bond has directed his own plays.

A director is a strange beast who is dependent on the creative power of the writer and the interpretative ability of the actor. He is a creation of the last hundred years or so; in the days of Molière and Shakespeare he didn't exist. Chekhov was the first major writer to suffer under a director, even though it was the Moscow Art Theatre that first made him a success. Every director is a frustrated writer in some way and if the play doesn't express what he wants it to, then the temptation is to make it do so in the production. I've tried to avoid this in my work but deep down in me lurks the same base desires as govern most directors. It's difficult to think of directing just as a journeyman job. A writer is constantly exposing his life, his political beliefs, his sexual fantasy, his moral standpoint and his sense of what theatre is. Has the director the right to do the same? Does he have any creative identity of his own?

My instinct is to say no. When I look at the work of 'Directors' Theatre' I am not only shocked but inexpressibly bored. The attempt to create images and concepts separately from the play makes for cumbersome and inelegant work. Plays last three times as long as any normal production to accommodate the directors' ideas (Patrice Chereau's *La Dispute* and Planchon's *George Dandin*) and the images are often banal in their violence or their sexuality. I believe that every play has an identity that it is the director's job to reveal. At the dress rehearsal of my first major Shakespeare production, *Richard III*, I had the sensation of this truth. I had just cut the Richard–Elizabeth scene to shorten a long evening and I was watching the play progress. The play stirred like some great monster on whose back we'd been running about and started to move forwards. It existed, with or without the scene; it had its own energy and life and rhythm apart from what we had done. Every moment of improvisation, every note, every inflexion had contributed only to letting the beast live. Since then I have never been able to believe that my own petty imaginings should be the basis of what is happening on the stage.

Jonathan Miller thinks it is impossible to know a writer's intentions and that it is not the director's business to try. I think this is plainly untrue. In his essay in 'To present the pretence' John Arden shows how a writer indicates what he wants to see on the stage without the use of stage directions.

Shakespeare means the ghost of Hamlet's father to be in full armour, wearing the visor of his helmet up, with a silvery grey beard and walking slowly. He has the recognizable presence of the dead king or how else can Hamlet say, 'I'll call thee king, Hamlet, father, royal Dane . . .'? The image is as much part of the writing as any line of dialogue. It's become fashionable, and I use the word advisedly, to make him some kind of vague symbol, a misty figure in the film speaking with Olivier's voice, something in Jonathan Pryce's stomach, a swirling curtain for Yuri Lyubimov. Anything but Hamlet's father. Something of the writer's intention has been changed. That is, the image has been changed but not the text, so one contradicts the other. The question is 'Do I find the director's imagination as powerful as Shakespeare's?' The answer is 'No.'

Two of the best productions I've ever seen were by the authors of the plays: Brecht's *Mother Courage* for the Berliner Ensemble and Beckett's *Waiting for Godot* for the Schiller Theater. Both were definitive and, as I found to my cost in the case of the Brecht, difficult for another director to follow. I don't believe that one has to go on endlessly imitating these productions, masterly though they were. But I do know that the director is on the quest of creating an experience for an audience of something that has already existed in the writer's mind. He is not creating something new. The whole area of performance art and non-literary theatre is something else. If all writers were qualified directors we would cease to exist. Many of our leading writers already direct their own plays but often lack the craftsmanship, the overall sense of theatre, the ability to combine the different strands which make up a performance.

In theory it makes obvious sense. Who knows the plays better than the writer? In practice there is sometimes a lack of resonance in the actors' work, a need for a life outside the text, which should be provided by the director. The private world of the writer, which should be made public by passing through the hands of others, is sustained in its privacy. Bond, and Howard Barker after him, have created a world difficult to enter and understand. Their work instead of reaching a larger audience is driven back into the small studio theatres. Bond's *The Woman* did surface on the Olivier stage, but I doubt that the experiment will be repeated. Both writers demand a serious and committed theatre, though I think neither would be happy with the same one, and castigate the existing institutions, particularly the Court, for not supplying it. They wander between the National and the RSC without really believing in either. There is an alienation between them and the stages on which they should be working, but there is an alienation between them and their potential public.

The lesson of the Court and of Joint Stock is that when the writer feels part of the theatre process, even if not actually attached to a building, his work will be better than if he wanders in isolation. Writers may need to detach themselves in order to write but if they sustain their existence and values apart from those of the people who present their plays, their work will become sterile and obscure.

None of this is possible without subsidy. It is sixteen years since I stopped being director of the Court and sixteen years before that the English Stage Company was founded. The first four years of my time coincided with Harold Wilson's first Labour Government and the liberal legislation that led to the end of censorship. It also coincided with an increased Arts Council grant in a time of economic expansion. Only thereafter was I dependent on transfers to the West End to finance experiments in Sloane Square. Since I left, first the recession and then years of Thatcherism have shrunk the Court's capacity to present full-scale work. Max Stafford-Clark, who took over in 1979, has made a virtue of this by importing the Joint Stock process to Sloane Square. A way of looking at theatre, which I had learned from George Devine, found new life outside the Court and has been brought back to where it was born. But for those of us who have moved on, the values we first learned there will continue to guide our work.

# Index